IT IS SOLVED BY WALKING

How World-Class Creators Solve Life

a bookito by
Evan Griffith

CONTENTS

For someone like you —

you know, who wants to go the distance

(and)

To Vegs, Ras and AnkaSeti —

The three people I've walked with most

(and)

To MomJo!

Who got us all moving early

i

WALK THIS WAY

(Aerosmith)

Pre-Amble, you could say

My hope for you in reading this bookito is that at some point you fling it aside. For what? To strike out for a walk....

Everything is within walking distance
if you have the time.

~ **Steven Wright**

Too many good things in my life have come from crisis, and I'm not happy about that

It was somewhere north of midnight, well north, 3 a.m. maybe. I awoke suddenly, ripped from sleep by fear and palpitations. My body thumped jackhammer speed from an unknown trauma. I was pinned between the dream realm and the waking world. The hybrid reality made no sense.

My heart sped. My breaths were shallow snorts. I moved to the couch nearby, attempting to breathe calmly, slowly, methodically. The panic only heightened. Was I … dying?

My torso was cold to the core, growing colder.

A death force oozed into the house, coming from the west, coming for me. It had already breached the far side of our home — I could sense it. I rose and shuffled into the bathroom, sat on the toilet feeling lightheaded, heart going so fast, too fast, feeling if I lost consciousness it would be the snuffing out of me. The death force vibrated inexorably in my direction. I prayed. Though not in the habit, prayer came easily. Dire circumstance will do that, focus you.

A thought came: Wake my wife! With her aid I might be able to escape this thing coming for me. If it reached me before I reached her it would be too late. I had to get to her first.

She put her hand on my chest. It beat as though a gorilla typist pounded with ape fists from inside. One of Ann's many gifts is the gift of calmness. Her hand on my chest, her soft ways, reassured me.

Off we went to the hospital, neatly evading the death force by exiting through the side door.

Good times.

— — —

Sometimes it takes seeing how others see you to instigate change. For me it wasn't impending death that really did it — it was a photo. It was a simple image a friend emailed me: Me standing next to a guy of some girth. What startled me was the convergence. He wasn't losing weight to match me. No, I had puffed out like a breakfast pastry. *I was gaining on him.* It was a shock. Was that doughy man really me?!

Lean lanky me had gone convincingly undercover.

There it was. It was undeniable. There's a continuum from fit to fat — I'd left the left axis of that graph far behind — I knew I had to do something.

After moving into a high-cost, high-promise location, our art gallery instead flailed as a slew of other businesses went bankrupt around us. It had been two years of unrelenting loss — and two years of physical neglect. Donuts and Dews and despair wreaked their havoc. More night terror episodes — or neurocardiogenic syndrome as the doctors called it — didn't quite act as the trip wire. To change, it also took seeing myself as the world saw me.

Thus began my walking program — 4.5 hours a week.

Solvitur ambulando

It is solved by walking

~ **Ancient Roman saying**

Ever so slowly in the aftermath of these night attacks, I undertook three initiatives:

1. Walking daily
2. Restricting my Mountain Dew intake to <u>two</u> a day (this is how far gone I was, that downing only two sodas a day was an improvement! I drink none a day now years later, baby steps)
3. A spiritual program centered around daily meditation, reading and giving in small ways

This bookito is inspired by the first. Walking.

Four and a half hours a week is 45 minutes a day with allowance for one day of sloth. Gots to have my slothday.

Quickie history

It is solved by walking.

St. Augustine first used the phrase to refer to a philosophical argument that is resolved by practical action. Specifically he was referring to Diogenes — that impish philosopher prankster — who, while listening to a presentation on one of Zeno's paradoxes attempting to prove that motion isn't real, gets up and walks away. Thus refuting Zeno's premise about the unreality of motion.

These Greek thinkers!

It is solved by walking. A philosophical debate is solved by practical experiment, in this case by merely moving. Diogenes gets up and walks away. Over the centuries that phrase penned by St. Augustine describing Diogenes' form of resolving a point of inquiry morphs its meaning. In time it becomes a literal statement. Originally not in the slightest meant as an endorsement of walking itself, *solvitur ambulando* — it is solved by walking — becomes a call to action for creators seeking to pull more from themselves.

It turns out so much more is solved by walking.

Something unexpected

Walking spurs more than bodily health. There are side effects no one warns you about. Because I didn't own any, I walked without head-phones, I walked without distraction. Just as when I walked often and on the merest impulse in earlier years, part of the appeal had always been getting lost in motion without anything artificial competing for my attention.

Unexpectedly this was the greatest gift I could give myself. It wasn't just vitality that came my way with the walking program, it was transfor-mation. The *so slow I didn't notice it at first* kind.

Small revelations popped to the surface. Often-times the thoughts should have been apparent … but it was only in slowing down that they coalesced. You don't realize until you walk how much the rest of your day is overload. There is always something tugging at you — sensations and information vie for your awareness. There's always something fighting for your focus.

Walking is a way to dispel all that.

Over time three broad categories of transformation beyond physical well-being emerged during my daily walks: Ideas, inspiration, and insight.

They may sound similar but they're not. Here's how I differentiate them:

<u>Ideas</u> — Little tweaks that leap to mind. Tiny advances that sneak in the back door of your brain. How we could improve a process. How I could squeeze out a better result in a particular art niche that seemed to be resonating in our market. How I could revisit a situation I'd handled poorly.

Simmering antagonisms became inconsequential as I plodded along for miles. Vexations resolved themselves. A new approach would suggest itself almost airily.

Why hadn't I thought of these solutions sooner?! Because I hadn't given myself over to silence. We are so keen on focus we forget unfocusing is as much a part of the equation. All those eurekas people have in the shower … they just needed a space for random thoughts to collide. That kind of randomness requires inattention.

Inspiration — These moments surge unexpectedly from the floor of your being. When inspiration arrives, a welling up of something primal overtakes you — suddenly the world feels buoyant, animated in every particle.

It's giddy making, these moments of connection. Enough to propel you forward into the chaos again, renewed.

You feel inspiration the way you feel love or hunger. Viscerally. It's less a thought, more an emotion, a whole body experience. Like you're inhaling divinity.

Insights — Here's an example: We were never going to make the gallery work in the current location. Yes, this should have been clear to me every day going into work, seeing one business after another belly up in front of us, but no, the clarity came during late night rambles. Everything clarifies when you walk without manufactured sound yammering in your ear.

You might wonder why I group insights and ideas into two categories. Aren't they essentially of one cloth? Yes and no. The difference between an idea and an insight is the difference between a burp and a sonic boom.

An idea is something to try, a tweak, an iteration, a *how about this?* An insight is seeing anew. You may discard an idea — it may or may not work — but an insight grows you. You perceive through fresh eyes.

For example, this insight changed how I looked at life:

For decades I bought into the worldview that everything of value takes hard work. It's a struggle, a slog — a long one — and eventually you attain Success.

Then an insight changed the way I looked at the world. It had to do with Ease — observing other people making advances *without struggle*.

Some people make painless shifts! And there was always a sense of Ease underlying them.

It didn't have to be a long hard slog to the solution. To the promotion. To the love of your life. To the opportunity that whisks you away from the unpleasant track you're on.

Often it was elan that brought you there: Liveliness. Artfulness. A side step. It might be a dash of irreverent pluck, using wit and a sharp mind in a line at Starbucks where you discover the person next to you is in a field of work that makes your heart beat a little faster. It could be lighthearted playfulness that helps one skate over the burdensome aspects of a job.

It could be something as simple as nonchalantly mentioning what you really want — and it catches the right ear — and voila, a door you didn't even know existed opens. You step through it into the new job, the new city, the new life, the new partner, the new digs — and you didn't get there because you sweated and grunted and groaned and worked under the hot desert sun for 35 years to get to where you wanted to be.

Oh, some people do. Yes. But most find Easeful transitions that loop them out of the slog. In fact, the most charmed among us have so constructed their lives that they embody it. They slip effortlessly from one activity to another.

When Jean-Jacques Rousseau had the epiphany that elevated him to one of the great 18th-century intellectuals — that civilized man had fallen from grace; it was the savage who lived nobly — he was walking several miles outside of Paris to visit a friend in prison, glancing through a newspaper.

There was Ease in that moment. And Insight. His life's work called to him then.

Oh, did you notice? He was walking.

(!)

Observing Easy transitions led me to question what I'm doing wrong each time life turns into a slog. Now when I become rutted I summon the Easy step. Or the Easier strategy. The one that will get me there more effortlessly.

I ask for it.

I ask myself in quiet moments. I'll ask in my Vision Pages that I write many a morning. I'll ask the incomprehensibly vast multiverse. I'll ask friends. Sheesh, if an inner prompting suggests it, I'll ask a stranger I've just met.

You can tell people on Easeful paths. They are filled with energy for what they do. They are propelled. In fact, the day energizes them. The work in front of them engages them, excites them, illuminates their lives even.

That was an insight — not an idea.

WORMHOLE TO CREATIVE INSIGHT

Now that I've hammered that point home — that ideas and insights are different in magnitude — I'm going to conflate them again in this section. The theme here — *walking is your wormhole to creative insight* — encompasses the spectrum from trifling to thrilling.

In advance, I'm not sure we can spawn an idea *or* insight at a designated time. But we can set up favorable conditions. The good news: The more you truck in ideas the more likely you are to be awash in insight too.

This section revels in this certainty: The simple act of walking conjures creative solutions, be they ideas or insights. Be they small test-it-in-a-minute changes in approach or mind-blowing my-God-this-changes-everything thunderclaps.

Among famous originals, what do you think is the most common means of spurring creative thought?

What would you imagine it to be? Drink? Drugs? Drama? Sex?

You know you want it to be one of those. I know I do, it makes for interesting reading … Even though I'm long past romanticizing it for myself, we suspect there's some kind of misery index at play. The greater the distress to the psyche, the greater the output of genius.

It wasn't until I larked through *Daily Rituals: How Artists Work* by Mason Currey that I was awestruck *by the myth* of great art requiring great pain.

It is solved by walking, say the ancients. You know who else says this? So many world-class creators in history your head spins. Nothing illuminates like a parade of work habits from dozens of humanity's greatest minds.

Over 150 creative titans are profiled by Currey, from choreographer Twyla Tharp to architect Frank Lloyd Wright to poet-autobiographer Maya Angelou to artist Pablo Picasso and so many more.

Two things stood out repeatedly in my reading, so much so they began to seem like the holy grail for all creatives:

1. Establish a creative routine
2. Take a walk

Setting up a creative routine seems to beg the obvious, though possibly only because of feverish Hollywood depictions regarding the artistic temperament, which might cause us to believe artists are wildly spontaneous and not given to establishing a work regimen.

In reality that would only be faux creatives. In the art world I inhabit, artistic individuals who want a career labor as determinedly as any would-be mogul. It was revelatory, reading *Daily Rituals*, to discover how many also find taking a walk essential to their creative genius.

It makes sense. Activity is good for the body-mind. Walking in particular is one of the few activities this side of yoga that is contemplative in nature.

Taking a walk is soul connecting ... and body flushing, flushing one's system of the detritus of the day. It's no wonder one of the simplest forms of movement is also one of the most en-riching.

The timeless practice world-class creators tap to solve problems, summon insight and spur vitality

Let me take you through a few snippets from *Daily Rituals* to inspire you:

Filmmaker Ingmar Bergman

In the late afternoon he went for a walk or took the ferry to a neighboring island ... "I never use drugs or alcohol," Bergman said. "The most I drink is a glass of wine and that makes me incredibly happy."

American composer Morton Feldman

I get up at six in the morning. I compose until eleven, then my day is over. I go out, I walk, tirelessly, for hours.

German composer Ludwig van Beethoven

After a midday dinner, Beethoven embarked on a long, vigorous walk, which would occupy much of the rest of the afternoon. He always carried a pencil and a couple of sheets of music in his pocket, to record chance musical thoughts.

Danish philosopher Soren Kierkegaard

Typically, he wrote in the morning, set off on a long walk through Copenhagen at noon, and then returned to his writing for the rest of the day and into the evening. The walks were where he had his best ideas...

Father of psychoanalysis Sigmund Freud

After dinner, Freud went for a walk around Vienna's Ringstrasse. This was not a leisurely stroll, however; his son, Martin, recalled, "My father marched at a terrific speed."

Every mystic's favorite psychologist
Carl Jung

[At his writing retreat] … He generally set aside two hours in the morning for concentrated writing. The rest of his day would be spent painting or meditating in his private study, going for long walks in the hills, receiving visitors, and replying to the never-ending stream of letters that arrived each day.

Viennese conductor and composer
Gustav Mahler

After lunch, Mahler would drag Alma on a three- or four-hour-long walk along the shore, stopping occasionally to jot down ideas in his notebook, beating time in the air with his pencil.

Writer William Faulkner

Then he would wake early, eat breakfast, and write at his desk all morning…. After a noon lunch, he would continue repairs on the house and take a long walk or go horseback riding.

Preacher and theologian Jonathan Edwards

To break up these long hours of private study, Edwards engaged in daily bouts of physical activity: chopping wood in the winter, walking or horse riding when the weather was good. On his walks, he carried a pen and ink to record his thoughts.

Writer Franz Kafka

… then ten minutes of exercises, naked at the open window [lucky Prague], then an hour's walk — alone, with Max, or with another friend….

Playwright Samuel Beckett

His entire life revolved around his almost psychotic obsession to write. The siege began with an epiphany. On a late-night walk near Dublin harbor, Beckett found himself standing on the end of a pier in the midst of a winter storm. Amid the howling wind and churning water, he suddenly realized that the "dark he had struggled to keep under" in his life — and in his writing, which had until then failed to find an audience or meet his own aspirations — should, in fact, be the source of his creative inspiration.

Walking is the unsung hero of the creative process — showers and post-coital reveries get all the press — driving even — but walks — oh walks — civilization owes a debt to you. Songs don't get sung about you — it ain't right —

On the importance of walking without sound in your ears

Walking with sound piped into your ears is an affront to clarity. And to absorption in the act of walking itself.

At first I was slow in putting this together. Sometime after I began my walking program I bought earbuds. I started listening to personal growth and spiritual audio programs. To do this occasionally will add novelty and knowledge. To do it habitually squelches originality. Your exquisite and singular creator self gets suppressed. Instead you are piping in the diktat of others, surrendering your thinking to what's been produced outside of you.

External stimuli overlays much of our day, to take this brief pocket of time and make it completely your own is an act of liberation. Like a fine tea you'll steep in yourself.

What about music, some might ask? In a different era this might have provoked a different response. Music is ubiquitous now. It's in your car or on your commute, in stores, in restaurants, even at work. It's in video games, on TV, in memes, in malls, in elevators and lobbies. It's on your computer and on your phone.

To walk without music or podcasts or audio of any kind is to unfetter your mind. Free yourself! Walk without bringing sound with you! Walk with you and your shallow thoughts! Walk with just you and your random mental flotsam. Walk with you.

When you walk with sound ported into your ears, you walk mesmerized, controlled by what others have created. This is not a bad thing from time to time. To sharpen your thoughts by tapping into the brainiacs who've tunneled seriously into a subject is the hallmark of civilization. It's bettering ourselves by accessing the refined creations of others.

But —

To do only this is to relinquish space for originality. Walking without artificial sound prompts brain play. Think of it this way:

Natural sounds coming to you randomly are gifts — nutrients enriching the soil from which your thoughts spring.

In time I came to understand this ... and made sure to free my mind to serendipity.

None of the notable creators mentioned earlier walked with sound piped in. True, all were from before the *sound at all times damn the silence* era we live in now. Even then, it's striking. Walking in silence, absorbing the ambient goings-on around you, letting your thoughts come undirected ... is one of the greatest recipes for insight there is.

Walking as creative fuel

Maria Popova, from the culture newsletter *Brain Pickings,* called it *walking as creative fuel* in the title of one of her email newsletters.

When you glance at historical creative thinkers who made a habit of walking, you find most engaged this activity after their intensive work had been accomplished. Can you think of a better time? You've exhausted yourself on the day's task. Brain and body are spent from immersive focus. You've been sitting at your desk locked in a non-yoga sitting pose at some length.

Time for a Mountain Dew? A toke off your hookah? Hardly. Time to get up, move, take in fresh air, letting the spill of life and nature and civilization surround you. Let your thoughts percolate in the background. Let vigor be your guide. Let a thousand disparate thoughts ramble and boink and leapfrog synaptic pathways.

The brain casts a wide net when the body is engaged in a narrow, low-impact activity. Blood flushes, brain cells spike with oxygen, toxins get squeezed out by lymphatic massage, it's beautiful what happens during a walk. Or any type of exercise for that matter.

For thinkers — for creators — walks in particular have an added bonus many types of exercise don't. Walking promotes a reverie that is paradoxically active and hypnotic. A walk is demanding enough to spark vitality yet low-key enough to let your mind play.

I swim and bike and do a little yoga. I've been a jump roper, a kayaker, a runner, a rock climber initiate (never progressing past white belt), a gym goer, and a sexlete in my own mind. The cognitive load is heavier for those activities. More focus is required. If you're not paying more attention while biking — whether urban, suburban or in nature — you're apt to pay for it in injury.

You won't be thinking of your novel climbing Annapurna. You won't be mulling product tweaks base jumping off the Burj Khalifa.

Walking is the oatmeal of creativity. With brown sugar on top. Simple, nutritious, requiring little mental energy. You free your mind in ways other pursuits don't allow.

You've freed your mind to what? To wherever it will go. To colonize Alpha Centauri. To pick over the day's detritus and build scaffolding for the rest of the week. To sift conversations and make yourself quippier next time. To scale the Denali of a relationship hurdle. To wade across the swamp of a personal failing to the other side.

To be.

As in meditation, the uni-direction of your pacing liberates. Walking itself is restorative, the way sitting erect and simply breathing is.

Walking shares this payoff with other low-engagement activities. Which is why train rides and naps provoke ideas. Idling outside on a park bench will do the same.

Waiting For Godot playwright Samuel Beckett wasn't rowing hard in a thrashing storm trying to evade drowning when the epiphany of his writing life came to him — that he should explore the chaotic darkness within him rather than suppress it — No, he was (safely) walking the length of a pier while storm waters raged below.

Walking prevails over other low-focus activities for one reason. Your body is engaged too. You're moving. You're breathing. You're outside of your normal confines. You're oxygen loading.

Even better, you're freestyling. When I head out for a walk I am no longer boxed in. I am no longer constrained by my expectations. I may be mulling over a creative impasse or a challenge at the gallery — but whatever concerns I set out with scamper off quickly. My mindstream becomes more like a mountain stream, touching upon this rock, that tree root, this bend, that puzzle, this possibility — it's inevitable the flow will lead me somewhere pleasant, maybe somewhere unexpected, if not exciting. But I won't know until I go!

Walking is — counterintuitively — creative fire. That's what you really want — a non-work activity that complements your life as an idea person. One that fuels you. Something that stokes your fire.

The concept that begat the 20th century

A young man, 19, acquires an obsession. Vital, asexual, athletic, he's a top student with a keen intellect, haunted by a new technology. In my youth it was software and personal computing, a decade and a half later it was the internet, now it is artificial intelligence and biotech and blockchain. In his time direct-current electricity was the new new thing. This was before lights you could flip on, before the telephone became widespread, before cars, before the age of plastics, before moon landings.

His is an anti-obsession. This student possessing more than a touch of arrogance revels in disputing his professor, who advocates for the direct current electricity transmission system then coming into vogue. The direct current motor is flawed — the young man knows it! — yet he can't muster a solution. He can feel it in the recesses of his mind — it's there, he can sense it.

Still a mechanical real-world solution eludes him.

He later wrote:

"I had so much energy to spare. When I undertook the task it was not with a resolve such as men often make. With me it was a sacred vow, a question of life and death. I knew that I would perish if I failed. Now I felt that the battle was won. Back in the deep recesses of the brain was the solution, but I could not yet give it outward expression."

He agonizes over his inability to draw forth a workable concept. Sleep becomes problematic, difficult. The university notifies his family, concerned the young man's lifestyle is killing him. No longer able to concentrate on his studies, obsessed with thoughts for an alternative motor, his routine breaks down. He imagines himself capable of seeing beyond ordinary men. Because he's far-seeing, untethered by common-man constraints, gambling becomes a means to his salvation — until he loses his tuition money and is forced to quit the university. Twenty-four-hour billiard stints and a losing streak at cards takes its toll.

His world splinters … A year later his father dies. He falls apart in slow motion over several years in several countries.

The now ex-student moves through a few Eastern European countries until he settles in Budapest, working for the new telephone industry springing up. His obsession with an alternative to the direct current motor revs up again.

In Budapest he suffers from a keen hypersensitivity. He's irritated by the ticking of clocks several rooms away — and the sound of trains miles away grates on him. He can't take it.

Something ruptures, he disintegrates. The young man becomes incapable of functioning. Though the term is no longer used medically — nervous breakdown — this is how his emotional collapse has been referred to historically. For a time it's feared he will die.

Once an avid hiker, in his recuperation he begins taking walks, cementing what will become a lifelong habit.

During his recovery late one afternoon, he walks with a friend to a city park. There, as he gazes at the sunset, he quotes Goethe's *Faust*. Nikola Tesla has a full-blown vision of a workable alternating current motor with oscillating magnets. Until then alternating current motors were laboratory curiosities, unable to compete with their direct current cousins.

The simplicity and ruggedness of Tesla's design would power the world.

On the spot Tesla roughed out a diagram in the sand for his friend.

Literature lovers might claim it was Goethe, cultural cross pollination. Nature lovers might claim it was the sunset, the park. Those who study creativity might claim it was immersion and release — immersion in his subject, with a break from the work to allow the brain to re-assemble patterns in the background.

I say it was all of it, facilitated by a walk.

Tesla's obsession with the faults of direct-current motors led to this breakthrough:

"At that age, I knew entire books by heart, word for word. One of these was Goethe's 'Faust'. The sun was just setting and reminded me of the glorious passage, 'Sie rückt und weicht, der Tag ist überlebt, Dort eilt sie hin und fordert neues Leben. Oh, da kein Flügel mich vom Boden hebt Ihr nach und immer nach zu streben! Ein schöner Traum indessen sie entweicht, Ach, au des Geistes Flügeln wird so leicht Kein körperlicher Flügel sich gesellen!' As I uttered these inspiring words the idea came like a flash of lightening and in an instant the truth was revealed. I drew with a stick on the sand, the diagram shown six years later in my address before the American Institute of Electrical Engineers, and my companion understood them perfectly.

"The images I saw were wonderfully sharp and clear and had the solidity of metal and stone, so much so that I told him, 'See my motor here;

watch me reverse it.' I cannot begin to describe
my emotions. Pygmalion seeing his statue come
to life could not have been more deeply moved.
A thousand secrets of nature which I might
have stumbled upon accidentally, I would have
given for that one which I had wrested from her
against all odds and at the peril of my exist-
ence..."

This sunny day in 1882 begat the 20th century.

Methinks that the moment my legs begin to move, my thoughts begin to flow.

~ Henry David Thoreau

Street walkers

Susan Claris, a British transport planner and anthropologist who advocates for walkable cities, says this about her own 50-minute walk to work:

"What I always find surprising is how much thinking you do when you are walking, without even meaning to," she says. "I always get ideas."

Yes!

"People always talk about the vitality of town centres; that's people." And by this she means people walking around. Not in buildings, not in cars, but physically on the streets.

Last summer our family drove to Taos, New Mexico, for the day. Once we disembarked from the van we walked the square and its offshoots. We were there — ostensibly — for the art. We own an art gallery — this is our Research and Development time. Every summer our family trip is organized around artists, those we represent and those we hope to serendipitously come across, whose work will speak to us so forcefully we'll want to represent them too.

When I read Susan Claris's observation — that vitality in city centers *is people* — people out and about — the obvious was made apparent to me. In our travels we seek out art destinations. We favor art towns, though cities are just fine too.

There's a particular flavor to our favorite locales. They're beautiful in idiosyncratic ways — Santa Fe nestled in the arid desert mountains; Carmel thick and green with Pacific ocean overspill — paradoxically they share commonalities. They tend to be intimate and contained. By this I mean they don't sprawl endlessly like L.A. or the Gobi desert. There's a definitive walking area. You can feel the perimeter as you near it, as if an invisible force field pushes you back around. It's not that something stops you — like a wall — or signs that say Go Back! — it's that you are no longer *pulled* forward. It could be a large open-air parking lot at the end of several walkable streets. A major artery with vehicles awhir. A change from retail to residential. A series of office buildings loom large and heavy on the streetscape you're traveling and you decide, oh, why don't we circle back. The absence of pull is where the walking area ends.

Buildings and spaces are often repurposed from an earlier era in art enclaves — like the Torpedo Factory in Old Town Alexandria, Virginia, once a building for munitions manufacture, now oozing with artists and galleries in every crevice — or the main drag in Bisbee, New Mexico, an artsy craftsy area reborn from Old West mining town roots.

There's a visceral feel to these art destinations. Traipse down Canyon Road in Santa Fe without seeing in your mind's eye cliff dwellers, Spanish missions, adobe huts, kivas afire, coyotes yipping and yowling, life and death over millennia in the high desert. You can't. The ancients whisper to you. What came before is embedded in the architecture. You can feel your way back past the Pueblo people to the Anasazi.

Yes, you may start with the New Age 70s and walk your way backward through the hippy 60s to the creative retreats begat in an earlier generation by Georgia O'Keefe and others … decades ceding to centuries, deleting the seekers, the artists, the westerners, the Spaniards, the human-hive-building Native Americans — you can strip away the architecture in your mind's eye, you just arrived from out of town, you know what the land looks like — stunted scrub and gnarled rock — you feel your way all the way back to footpaths, to hunting by spear and atlatl. It's there in the landscape. Before horses came with the Europeans, dogs bore the heavy labor of transport, pulling loads by sled. Without wheels! You may not be up on the history — you've only just arrived — yet you feel it in you.

Or you're in La Jolla, outside of San Diego, where the streets skirt cliffs at the edge of the continent. Your view plunges to the Pacific in spots, salt spray permeates the air on tumultuous days, Southern California affluence unrolls before you at every turn. Avocado is on the menu in some variation nearby.

These art towns can range from the bejeweled and lovely to the rangy and crusty. The denser the pedestrian traffic the more likely it traffics in craft, not art. Take St. Augustine in northeast Florida. It's primary shopping via is so popular a tourist destination, art can't thrive there. Only goods sold at lower price points. Something that will only take minutes to decide upon.

To walk the cobblestone alley in St. Augustine is to hark back to conquistadors and smithies and tanneries. Clayware and fabrics, mugs and t-shirts, jewelry and ice cream are best sold in tourist destinations.

They all have vitality in common. People. In full flux, moving and roving about on their own accord, not a mechanized vehicle extant save perhaps the occasional scooter for the impaired.

People strolling, people milling about, some purposeful, some idling, some bored, some fascinated, people peopling up the sidewalks and eateries, flowing in rivulets down the streets, eddying into an ice cream shop, pooling at an outdoor cafe. We want to be among people! Not people in cars or people in subways or people in planes. To go into town — or out on the town — is to crave the most fleeting of connections with humanity, the kind that can only be had in crowds. We want to people watch. We want to be participant and observer.

Maybe it's the tribal instinct still alive in us. To walk among others is a high state of connection.

It's what art towns and shopping districts and green markets have in common.

People.

Walking.

Nomad in Paris

No one drives in a great city. Can you imagine driving through Manhattan, thinking you've experienced it in any meaningful way? Same with San Francisco, London, Tokyo, Sydney, Hong Kong, Marrakesh. A great city requires real effort, it requires this of you: That you abandon your car. That you step off the train. That you set foot in it to explore it.

Didn't Henry Miller tramp endlessly through Paris? *Tropic of Cancer* was an extended howl from his vagabond days in France's capital city, the capital of the cultural world at the time.

One of my favorite lines from all of literature is embedded within that book:

"I have no money, no resources, no hopes.
I am the happiest man alive."

~ Henry Miller

That sentiment perfectly expresses the unexpected buoyancy one achieves when all is cast off. It also hints at the surprising transcendence that can unspool from loss. Of one's employment, one's country, one's marriage. Miller came to this understanding roaming the streets of Paris for hours.

If you go to Paris and sit on a park bench in an old section of the city, it's quite possible it's been there a hundred years or more. Meaning, where your buttocks spread comfortably, chances are Henry Miller's did too. He parked himself on benches often, scribbling notes, taking respite from his wanderings, plotting how to cajole a meal from his friends.

(Miller set up an ingenious program. He invited himself to weekly meals with various acquaintances. Monday night would be one, Tuesday another, and so on. He'd starve all day and gorge himself silly that evening, swiping bread and such for the morrow. A perfect meal plan for an urban nomad, one who preferred whiling away his hours on his own to working a job.

His comrades never suspected. Or more likely, were happy to oblige for a time. Until he snuck off with the wife or ranted a little too often against the drudgeries of the working stiff, the one whose job provided the meal.)

Miller also penned this, ostensibly about writing but at its core, about idea generation:

> "After all, most writing is done away from the typewriter, away from the desk. I'd say it occurs in the quiet, silent moments, while you're walking or shaving or playing a game, or whatever, or even talking to someone you're not vitally interested in."

Urban creatives

A friend said this of modernist poet Wallace Stevens, about coming from Connecticut to Manhattan:

"Sometimes he'd come down and he'd just walk around by himself. He loved to walk."

At home in Hartford, Stevens walked the 2.4 mile trip to and from his office every day. He often composed poetry en route. Though a wealthy insurance executive, he never learned to drive — these daily walks in all seasons were perhaps a factor in Stevens eventually winning the Pulitzer Prize for Poetry. They gave him the space to think.

Stevens composed on slips of paper during his walks, handing them to his secretary to type up. Some might see this as theft of company re-sources, yet Hartford Accident And Indemnity Company can now lay claim to aiding and abet-ting modern poetry, rebalancing the scales somewhat.

You know who else was a tremendous walker? Victorian novelist Charles Dickens, whose novels gave us characters like Scrooge and the lame pure-hearted Tiny Tim, whose stories inspired reform in an era of great social disparity.

Dickens often felt it necessary to walk as many hours as he wrote, sniffing out inspiration for plot points during his London walks. He tended to set out at night, calling the city his *magic lantern*, the term evoking how gaslit city streets illuminated his thoughts, the sights conjuring characters and scenes.

Dickens even wrote a short piece titled "Night Walks," about lengthy ramblings on foot extending into the early morning hours during a period of insomnia.

Christian philosopher Soren Kierkegaard, considered the originator of existentialism, stalked the streets of Copenhagen daily. He reveled in its crooked streets, where the laborers and the destitute and the wealthy intermingled.

Kierkegaard's great daily pleasure seems to have been walking the streets of his city. It was a way to be among people for a man who could not be with them, a way to bask in the faint human warmth of brief encounters, acquaintances' greetings, and overheard conversations....

Walking provided Kierkegaard, like Rousseau, with a wealth of casual contacts with his fellow humans, and it facilitated contemplation.

~ From *Wanderlust: A History of Walking* by the formidable Rebecca Solnit

A walking habit — daily constitutionals as they were once called — appears to have played a significant part in the deep creative work of many a historical figure. Motion and solitude together pack a powerful punch, discharging insights and solutions that might not come as readily while engaged in the actual work.

Walking is a siesta for the neocortex. As the higher brain functions throttle down, thoughts jostle in the background. It's a potent mix. Many an epiphany explodes into view under these conditions.

It's a modern thing too. Check this out — this is Time Magazine's Eliza Berman speaking of writer-director-actor Greta Gerwig during an interview:

After lunch in the West Village, she suggested—on this frigid February day, with flurries swirling about and a doggie bag of half-eaten pasta Bolognese in her backpack—that we trek across the island, and then a bridge, before she heads to pedestrian-averse Los Angeles the next day. Gerwig likes to walk, often as a remedy for writer's block. It's when you're walking, she insists, that life happens to you.

Bukowski: A theory

Time Magazine called him a "laureate of American low life."

I have a pet theory: That underground poet-novelist Charles Bukowski first learned how to become a functional alcoholic through urban walking. He gave up writing for a decade; he called it his 'ten-year drunk." I quit for 15! — though drinking wasn't involved, so maybe that doesn't count. Quitting your creative work to frenetically build a struggling art gallery doesn't have the same cultural resonance as despair, wantonness, ennui….

During this hiatus from his creative work Bukowski joined the post office. After hospitalization and near-death from a bleeding ulcer, he began writing again.

Drinking too, but hey, probably in a more moderated manner since he lived for decades more.

Bukowski plodded away at the postal service for years. One wonders if that alone helped him with his creative output, a counterforce to the drinking. Could the walking have been an antidote to his alcoholism? He belly ached mightily about being on his feet all day in *Post Office*, his first novel. Could walking have sparked his imagination while shuffling the city streets?

If so, Thank you, U.S. Post Office! Like others admired in one's youth, his work might not appeal to me now. It doesn't matter. Bukowski's dirty realism jiggles many a post-adolescent brain with its emphasis on bodily function and crass pursuits. If that's you, you probably have walking to thank for that.

Goethe: A man!

Goethe's penchant for walking to exhaustion helped maintain his physique to such an extent Napoleon, upon first meeting him, looked up and exclaimed: "You are a man!"

Already in his late 50s when they first met — my age! — Johann Goethe exuded the kind of quiet magnetism we'd all like to cultivate.

You are a man.

Who doesn't want to hear that from a young emperor, even if self-proclaimed?

It's not the same as *You are the man!,* which came into vogue in the late 90s. You could be *the man!* simply for spiking alcohol content in party punch — expediting paperwork — leveling up in a videogame — replying in a timely manner to an email.

To be an exemplar for all men, however ... *You are a man!* implies intellectual vigor, robust physicality. Who doesn't want that?

Adventurous walking and a questioning mind — certainly in tandem — helped Goethe earn this epithet.

After their meeting, Napoleon turned to an acquaintance, uttering: "There is a man for you."

Goethe had it all....

Intellectual heft (he'd worked at applied engineering in mining)

Creative daring (Goethe's *The Sorrows of Young Werther* had beguiled Napoleon, who'd reportedly read that novel seven times — it tells the story of a young man spurned by love who ultimately commits suicide)

Royal position (he was summoned to the Weimar Republic by a young Duke Karl August, retaining a lifelong position at the court)

And an international reputation as a multifaceted genius, as capable in letters as he was in botany, optics, anatomy and engineering.

A true Renaissance man.

Had these accomplishments been presented to Napoleon in the form of a flabby pastry of quasi-maleness, it's doubtful the military strategist would have been so impressed. Napoleon had met many of the finest minds of the continent. It was a pastime of his, to engage in conversation with the keen intellects of the era. Instead Goethe came hearty and hale, still vital despite his advancing years.

Goethe's primary mode of exercise from what we can gather was hiking. Tramping for hours up and down hills, roads, pathways and mountainsides. He collected rocks and minerals and fossils in his walks, the way you and I might collect seashells along the shoreline. By the thousands.

Goethe explored cities with similar aggression, enjoining friends and acquaintances to walk with him at every opportunity. Though he did seem to harbor a preference for a certain type of walking companion....

As Joseph McCabe in *Goethe, The Man And His Character* writes:

It is clear, however, that one of Goethe's most pleasant distractions was taking walks with pretty and charming maidens.

Epiphanies on the way to somewhere

Saul, persecutor of Christians, had such a profound vision while walking to Damascus he changed his name. To Paul. (Rhymes with the old one.) He repudiated his former path, transforming a splinter sect into a formidable religion, becoming Christianity's greatest advocate and second most important figure after Jesus, virtually a co-founder. Though, like Steve Wozniak, the other guy gets all the glory.

In the summer of 1881 while skirting the edge of a lake in Switzerland, Friedrich Nietzsche hit upon one of the more striking thought experiments in philosophy: Infinite return (aka infinite recurrence), because one is asked to imagine you will repeat your life exactly as it has been lived, returning to the same moments again and again, throughout eternity.

Implied in this scenario is this question: If you were forced to relive your life identically, moment by moment — time after time — would you be crushed or exalted?

Daniel Kahneman won a Nobel Prize for work he developed with Amos Tversky over many extended daily walks. Prospect theory, which led to behavioral economics, was born from two collaborators walking and talking: Two thinkers puzzling out the interconnection between cognitive psychology and economic decisions. (Contrary to classical economics' assumption of rational choice making, behavioral economics suggests there's a surprising *lack of reasoning* going on in human decision making. So don't feel badly about that time-share investment you can't shake.)

At 60 years of age actress and author Shirley MacLaine trekked the Camino de Santiago. To her the most poignant lessons came after the journey. Because each day's walk demanded so much physically, she discovered it was only after such a pilgrimage that the deepest insights from the trip emerged.

(A side note that relates not at all to walking: I'm forever indebted to MacLaine for introducing me in one of her early books to the idea of baths as a spiritual practice. In the text she referred to her evening baths as her spiritual time — I, a young lad in his late teens or early twenties, had a hearty laugh. *Ahhhh Hollywood!* Methought, *Only you can take luxury and make it a quasi-religious experience.* Skip forward a few years, one night in a bathtub I discovered how right MacLaine was — baths are ideal for reflection, for deepening one's commitments!)

Isaac Newton claimed his theory of gravity was spurred by watching an apple fall while meandering outdoors, in nature. The theory was not born full cloth from that episode — Newton had already been consumed with the motion of heavenly bodies. Yet witnessing an apple fall caused him to ask questions: *Why did it always fall down? And not sideways or upward?*

Because Newton was sequestered at his family home in the country for two years while the plague swept through Europe, he had time to contemplate answers. And to extrapolate further: *If a force affected an apple, why not something higher, even indeed the moon?* From there he meticulously mapped out formulas that became the groundwork for the scientific revolution of the next 300 years. Thank you for our modern era, Newton. Thank you, apple. Thank you, outdoors ramble.

Walking meetings

It's the rage in Silicon Valley.

Like nerf gun wars in the workplace, sleep pods for naps to keep you productive and casual Fridays every day of the week, one can only hope this trend goes nationwide. The technorati have taken walking to a whole other level: We're not talking just walking, we're talking *walking meetings*.

Though they didn't begin with Steve Jobs, his iconic commitment to walking meetings elevated the concept to a Best Practices discipline for the C Suite. For exercise. For ideas. To work out a problem. And especially to engage in deep dialogue.

Biographer Walter Isaacson on the Apple impresario:

"Taking a long walk was his preferred way to have a serious conversation."

Steve Jobs was most frequently seen walking around the Apple campus with product designer Jony Ives, hashing out details. They were together so often fellow workers gave them a conjoined name, as though they were a celebrity couple: Jives …

Jobs told Isaacson,"If I had a spiritual partner at Apple, it's Jony."

Walking and obsessing over issues large and small would naturally spill over into personal revelations. You can imagine how hundreds of hours of walks would cement such a relationship, making it more mindmeld than workaday.

The tech world has been inspired by Jobs in this area:

Facebook founder Mark Zuckerberg, Twitter co-founder Jack Dorsey and Google CEO Sundar Pichai are all famously fond of walking meetings. It's not only the tech titans. Barack Obama likes them too, often taking walking meetings when he could.

Decades ago billionaire Richard Branson came to a similar conclusion. That short walking meetings produce clearer action points. Branson prefers short meetings standing up. A walking meeting is even better.

Branson wrote in his blog:

When given the opportunity I often like to take things a step further – literally, with a walking meeting. I sometimes even set myself a personal challenge of trying to come up with a plan of attack in the time it takes to walk around the block... five minutes, go!

Phone walks

I have a variant on the walking meeting: The walking phone call. When I need to make a call to an artist or associate, friend or family member, I like to get up for a short walk.

Sometimes I'm up and circling about my office several times a day. That adds up. You know what helps? Keeping a small pad and pen with me. This way I don't feel tethered to a computer. I can strike out — bravely — adventurously — away from my desk — knowing I can jot down any info that needs to be stored.

It's restorative, these phone walks. They may be short in duration but my lymph system thanks me. My brain gets an extra dose of oxygenated nutrient-rich plasma. My body purrs like a cat after a good stretch.

Let's pause for a public service announcement:

- None of this refers to walking while visually engaged with your phone!
- Texting, messaging in any form, or playing with your device while walking results in thousands of deaths a year.
- If you are in an urban environment, choose a hallway or corridor or park for your walking calls.
- City sidewalks and streets can be lethal to the distracted walker.
- (This includes you, with music in your ears, with podcasts murmuring, with audiobooks intoning.)

My friend Gil paces when on a call. Many do. I do too. Often ambling out of headset range while my phone idles on my desk. Nothing shouts *Turn back!* like a suddenly staticky voice dropping into a void of nothingness.

The last half of that sentence ends on existential uplift, doesn't it — we'll bring in Mark Twain to lighten the moment.

(As this bookito goes to publication the coronavirus pandemic has hit the world. Phone walks are more important than ever. With business associates and friends and family. I've been scheduling phone walks with as many as I can, to keep in touch, to stay healthy, to get outdoors in a time of indoor isolation.)

Twain and Twitchell

While living in Hartford, Connecticut, Mark Twain and his good friend Reverend Joe Twitchell took Sunday jaunts to a tower on Talcott Mountain, approximately five miles out of town. Average walking speed is 3.1 miles per hour — for humans. A little faster for goats without packs, slower for sloths with or without packs.

This means Twain and Twitchell probably spent around four hours each weekend getting to and from the tower, including a short respite upon arrival. Robust Joe Twitchell may have sped up the pace a bit. These friends weren't comrades in arms, they were comrades in feets. An afternoon of walking and talking is bound to forge affinity — and prompt far ranging topics.

Their close friendship spanned four decades.

During his Civil War days as a young Union Army chaplain, Twitchell amused himself by 'developing radicalisms' to speak to Rebel prisoners. One was his "hope and confidence that I would live to see a negro President of the U.S.' (Had he lived another ninety-some-odd years beyond his death in 1918 he would have seen his wish come true.)

An athletic sort, Twitchell would often carry two or three men's gear while marching, to help those who'd fallen ill. He has been described as having an "exuberant sense of humor" and a lifelong commitment to social causes.

These qualities endeared Twitchell to everyone's favorite humorist, who himself evolved to more progressive ideals as he aged. (Anti-slavery, anti-war, anti-animal cruelty, anti-eggheadedness, anti-imperialist, pro-women's rights, pro-laissez faire economics *and* pro-labor union, whoa hoa, imagine!)

In a notebook Twain wrote this: *The radical of one century is the conservative of the next. The radical invents the views. When he has worn them out the conservative adopts them.*

After a successful article in *The Atlantic Monthly,* editor William Dean Howells asked Mark Twain for another article but he came up dry. Until, that is, he went for one of the 10-plus-mile walks with Twitchell.

Twain reminisced about his days on the Mississippi, telling stories of steamboats, their crews, their passengers, marking twain (measuring depth of water), the gamblers, the women — he was coming of age then, after all. On one walk Twitchell suggested to Twain that he 'hurl' his steamboat memories into an article.

This chat amongst friends begat what many think of as Mark Twain's finest work outside of his fiction: His steamboat series, first called *Old Times On The Mississippi,* then later expanded to become a 600-page book titled simply *Life On The Mississippi.*

This series of articles was the pivot point, when Twain's work began its evolution from playing for laughs to full-throated literature.

Creation walks

In an essay full of pith and insight on the benefits of a long walk, Arianna Huffington notes that Ernest Hemingway would resolve issues in his work by taking walks on pathways along a river. (Links to this article and other sources mentioned in this bookito are provided in the Resources section at the end.)

Huffington quotes from *A Moveable Feast*, about Hemingway's time in Paris:

"I would walk along the quais when I had finished work or when I was trying to think something out. It was easier to think if I was walking and doing something or seeing people doing something that they understood."

In an article on creativity at QZ.com by Davis Kadavy:

In 1891, German scientist Hermann von Helmholtz—whose accomplishments included inventing the ophthalmoscope—was honored with a party for his 70th birthday. He got up to make a speech, and shared how he achieved his creative insights:

"Often … [ideas] arrived suddenly, without any effort on my part, like an inspiration…. They never came to a fatigued brain and never at the writing desk. It was always necessary, first of all, that I should have turned my problem over on all sides to such an extent that I had all its angles and complexities 'in my head.' … Then … there must come an hour of complete physical freshness and quiet well-being, before the good ideas arrived. Often they were there in the morning when I first awoke…. But they liked especially to make their appearance while I was taking an easy walk over wooded hills in sunny weather."

An easy way to try this on your own is to engage in a creation walk. Take any experience you wish to enjoy and walk it into existence. Take the imagined experience with you as you set out. Play with it in your mind. What would it feel like if it came to fruition?

The book, the app, the bod, the project, the apartment, the lover, the trip, the job, the scene, the presentation, the perfect night out, the voice, the look, the hairstyle, the art style, the architectural style, the lifestyle. What might it look like when it comes blowing into your life in its full glory?

What might it *feel* like?

Tease out details that would delight you.

While you walk, let your mind romp in the direction of your desired experience. Never mind how you'll get there. Ignore the *cursed hows*, as Mike Dooley is fond of saying. It's more important to know where you're headed than how.

Playfully construct what you want while you walk, knowing that the means to that end will present themselves to you — in actions to take, and satisfyingly, in circumstances that open up in ways you couldn't have imagined, with people sliding effortlessly into your path at just the right nexus points.

Like every good creation, once you've tired of the game, let it go. Release it to the wind; release it to the infinite sky above. Walk on. Enjoy yourself, dammit. What you need will come in another hour, another moment, another day. Once you've dreamed, you've done enough.

Creation walks are all about conjuring. Ideas will come…. What you need will come….

On many occasions as an artist,
I have solved a painting by taking a walk.

~ Charlotte Hutson Wrenn

Artist, South Carolina low country lover

Out your front door

Stuck for ideas? Walk out your front door. There is a yawning expanse waiting for you.

The other day I witnessed continental drift theory in action in a cloud. Pangaea in the sky split apart. First rifts, then peninsulas and finally the great cloud itself was torn apart. I saw continents form and float away from the original mass.

You might see ducks waddling across the sky — or the resolution to a perplexing issue.

All the ideas you seek are out your front door.

THE BODY-MIND HYPERLOOP

There's something about
the rhythm of walking,
how, after about an hour and a half,
the mind and body can't help getting in sync.

~ Bjork

Toxins be gone

Toxins can only be removed by your lymph system through motion. The lymph system has no pump of its own. This system — the one that enhances your immunity and removes cellular waste from your bod — has no heart to pulse its fluids, no lungs to flush its contents, no bowels to push its load merrily along. It requires external motion.

It's not sitting in a car doing 70 mph kind of motion we're talking about. Nope, your body needs to be moving. Your body needs action the way a baby needs love — the way you and I need love! — throughout waking hours.

Nature is clever. It engineered a system — the lymphatic system — without an internal engine. It borrowed from all the energy going on around it. Muscles flexing, limbs swinging, spine articulating, torso contorting. Throughout all of human history up to about, oh, your grandparents era, people moved so much in the course of a day the lymph system had a free ride. The lymph system was happy go lucky. It was plucky in its ingenuity, riding the energy cascades of active lifestyles across the planet.

Think hunting, gathering, fishing, farming, working at manual or factory labor, cleaning, cooking, chopping, sweeping, child rearing without screens….

Then sitting became the thing. Feel free to boo and hiss. Even better if you do it standing up. You've shown real chutzpah if you strode across the room, flung open the air-conditioned window and shouted into the car-clogged streets: "Down with sitting!"

(Says he who is writing these words contentedly plunked in a mesh chair, feet up, gazing out open sliding doors at the rainstorm unfurling a couple yards away. *Go, Nature, go!* I'm emoting.)

(Did I walk at any time in the last three days? No. But I de-hoarded my Mom's home for hours on end. Lymph nodes are in near bliss, akin to a drug high.)

Walking speed and longevity

Want to know how long you're going to live? Me too, though not to the day, it would make getting to sleep the night before problematic.

If so, here's some interesting intel from an article in Scientific American Magazine:

A new analysis *of walking speed studies shows that—down to the tenth of a meter per second—an older person's pace, along with their age and gender, can predict their life expectancy just as well as the complex battery of other health indicators.*

So instead of a doctor assessing a patient's blood pressure, body mass index, chronic conditions, hospitalization and smoking history and use of mobility aids to estimate survival, a lab assistant could simply time the patient walking a few meters and predict just as accurately the person's likelihood of living five or 10 more years—as well as a median life expectancy.

This analysis pooled together 9 studies on older populations. I don't know about you, but reading this has made me pick up my pace.

10,000? Is that what you really need?

Even more exciting, another study that followed adults in their seventies for eight years found daily walking *decreases* mental decline and *increases* the amount of gray matter in your brain. Less cognitive deterioration and more of the brain matter that matters. From something as simple as taking a walk every day.

Let's pause to celebrate that — for the low cost of a walk a day you'll stay mentally alert longer in old age. Can I get a *Hell Yes!?*

For those of you addicted to your fitbits and fitness trackers, you'll want to know this — the magic number is 8,900. That number of footsteps a day makes you a demigod — at least in relation to your inactive peers. It's the threshold to superhealth.

What a relief for you 10,000 steps-a-dayers who don't quite make the mark. 8,900 will do just fine. 8,899 not so much.

(Kidding!)

What is that, 8,900 steps? That's walking for about an hour and a half a day. The study measured the cumulative number of steps each day — not just when people went out for a walk. This includes housework, shopping, pacing on the phone (see earlier segment), walking to and from your car, letting the damn dog out yet again, getting up for a glass of water — or a snifter of brandy — the pedometer was agnostic as to intent. It clocked it all. Except maybe night runs to the bathroom — who'd still be wearing their pedometer then?

Are you curious about the origin or the 10,000-steps-a-day rule? After researching it late one night I turned to my wife.

Me: *Wow, how do you think the 10,000 step rule came about?*

Ann, drowsily, tongue in cheek: *Hmmmmm, Malcolm Gladwell?*

Harvard Professor I-Men Lee was curious too. Turns out it was to sell a product! A Japanese pedometer company in the 1960s named their device the 10,000 Step Meter because the Japanese character signifying 10,000 looks vaguely like a person walking. The lack of rigor behind this cultural meme about daily walking goals prompted Lee to do what curious scientific minds do everywhere: Start a study.

Mercifully Lee's study gives us even more leeway: 4,400 was the number of steps a day that proved to significantly boost vitality/longevity. With the benefits accruing for additional steps daily, up to around 7,500. After that it was a wash, the additional steps per day didn't move the dial statistically.

There's even good news for the exercise disinclined: Even as few as 2,000 steps a day provides health benefits. You're just not going to set any lifespan records at that rate — no happy centennial for you.

Tremble not, though, you who don't want to walk so much. Because all exercise helps your brain, you'll be heartened to hear that short bouts of exercise prime your brain cells for learning. Any exercise.

The moral of the story here is mix your exercise like your salads. Like I mix my metaphors. Walking can be your greens. Everything else makes your bod and brain even better.

My grandmother started walking five miles a day when she was sixty. She's ninety-seven now, and we don't know where the hell she is.

~ Ellen DeGeneres

Sitting disease — and its antidote

Have you come across this new saying prevalent in the health arena the last few years? *Sitting is the new smoking.*

There's a new new term that encapsulates it further: *Sitting disease.*

The right pithy phrase can knock us upside the head, forcing us to take note of an issue. Disease, ugh. From sitting? It makes sense if we're inactive *all the time* that it's going to eventually incapacitate us. That's why so many of us exercise at the end of the day — or the beginning of the day.

"The more you sit the higher the risk of mortality even if you attempt to mitigate the effect with moderate-vigorous exercise."

~ From a 2012 study including more than 240,000 people

Alarmingly, prolonged sedentariness — sitting while you work all day, and then more for your commute, and some more for dinner, and even more sittingness as you're entertained by TV or tablet, console or computer screen — can't be counteracted by one bout of exercise.

In an article titled *Sitting Disease Is The New Health Hazard*, Dr. Erik Peper details the results of an 8.5 year study following more than 240,000 adults over 50. The surprise? That even moderately vigorous exercise once a day cannot fully erase the harmful effects of too much sitting.

What are some of these harmful effects, you ask?

Let's pull up **a partial list of the ill effects of prolonged sitting**:

—   **Toxic buildup**: Without frequent movement the lymph system has no motion to borrow for its cleaning process
—   Lower energy expenditure means **weight gain** if caloric intake isn't dropping commensurately

— **Slower metabolism**, which reduces the amount of fats removed from the bloodstream
— **Back strains** and **pains from immobility**
— **Musculo-skeletal warpage** due to lack of use, which can lead to chronic pain
— **Loneliness** or **depression**, from lack of social interaction, lack of exposure to fresh air and sun (with its dose of Vitamin D, among other benefits)
— **Incidence of cancer** increases with sedentary lifestyles
— **Heart disease** or **stroke**
— **High blood pressure**
— **High blood sugar**
— Increased risk of **diabetes**
— Increased **anxiety**
— **Deep vein thrombosis**, a smart term meaning a blood clot in your leg
— **Varicose veins** or spider veins. Where blood pools in your legs causing the veins to twist and bulge out
— **Osteoporosis** (weakened bones)
— **You're more likely to die earlier *of any cause*** the longer you are sedentary each day

And this is a partial list. Scientists aren't even sure why extended inactivity amps up the probability for some of these issues — they just know that it does.

The simplest antidote to our modern era's sitting disease is the quick walkabout. Simply getting up and walking a short distance and then returning. Five minutes! Three minutes. One minute even.

You can slap gold stars on your fridge if you do even more:

— Walk a short distance *and then stretch*. Then return.
— Walk a short distance *and then boogie oogie oogie*. Then return.
— Walk a short distance *and then strike a yoga pose*. Then return.
— Walk a short distance *and then do pushups. Or lunges*. Then return.
— Walk a short distance *and then insult someone so effectively you have to turn tail and run*. In this scenario, you may not be able to return.

— Walk a short distance *and then ... whatever your heart desires.* Then return.

All those bad bad things in the Bad List above? They can be avoided by simply moving a wee bit — often — throughout your day.

Breaking up your day with (brief) pacing or (short) walks is the easiest breeziest medicine there is to prevent a host of negative effects you don't want visited upon you.

The good news is better than the bad news

Ready for good news? A single bout of exercise brings on such good benefits memes should be flying in your feed all day long about it. Researchers call a one-time round of movement *acute exercise*. When we normally hear *acute*, we think, Uh oh, that's not good — maybe it's even nasty bad.

He died of acute alcohol poisoning.

San Francisco has an acute housing crisis.

She'd hoped it was acute dress, but alas, no.

No one wants acute psoriasis or acute flatulence or even acute halitosis for that matter. But in this instance — acute exercise — *acute* simply means *a single instance of.*

In the research, acute exercise often refers to walking, but it can be any movement, from low to high intensity depending upon the study.

I hear you calling out, I hear your demands. Previously we listed a bunch of negative effects from daily prolonged sitting. Now you crave a Good List and you're getting vocal about it. Simmer down, it's coming.

Your wish is granted. Here's **a partial list of what a single bit of exercise can do for you**:

— Eliminate toxins, yay!
— Enhance mood
— Reduce confusion
— Lessen anger
— Reduce fatigue
— Improve brain function (you're more creative, solve problems easier and gain better recall)
— Improve vital organs function
— Reduce stress
— Increase attention
— Improve verbal fluency

And if you walk or exercise as little as three or four times a week, the Good List multiplies like Tribbles:

— Diabetes patients reduce the progression of their disease by more than 50%

- Frequent walking also reduces the risk of developing adult-onset diabetes in the first place
- Post-menopausal women reduce hip fractures by 41% (woah, that's a lot for 4 walks a week)
- People diagnosed with depression find significant relief
- Knee pain is reduced for 47% of arthritic knee-joint sufferers
- Improves overall cardiovascular health
- Which also means it reduces coronary heart disease
- Reduces blood pressure
- Reduces risk of stroke
- Boosts mental and emotional health
- Burns fat/helps with weight loss
- Reduces risk of a variety of cancers
- Lowers insulin resistance
- Improves digestion (especially if post-meal walks are taken)
- Expands lung capacity (breathing better is good!)
- Increases bone strength
- Improves balance
- Stimulates overall energy
- Lessens anxiety
- Improves overall health

—   Improves overall brain functioning

There's more, but let's end on those last two — those are sufficient to get me up and out of my chair right now, to head out for a walk. See ya! I'll be back in a bit …

The best pill there is

From an article in Harvard Magazine by Jonathan Shaw:

"In the bottle before you is a pill, a marvel of modern medicine that will regulate gene transcription throughout your body, helping prevent heart disease, stroke, diabetes, obesity, and 12 kinds of cancer — plus gallstones and diverticulitis.

Expect the pill to improve your strength and balance as well as your blood lipid profile. Your bones will become stronger. You'll grow new capillaries in your heart, your skeletal muscles, and your brain, improving blood flow and the delivery of oxygen and nutrients. Your attention span will increase.

If you have arthritis, your symptoms will improve. The pill will help you regulate your appetite and you'll probably find you prefer healthier foods. You'll feel better, younger even, and you will test younger according to a variety of physiologic measures. Your blood volume will increase, and you'll burn fats better. Even your immune system will be stimulated. There is just one catch.

There's no such pill. The prescription is exercise."

And the easiest simplest most transcendent physical practice is walking.

I advocate for walking with poles. We'll get there in a minute.

Transformation stories abound

Perform even the shallowest of Internet searches and you'll trip over transformation stories through walking. There are sites and programs dedicated to walking for weight loss. Real life examples abound. With photos to prove it. There's nothing like seeing a person's physicality transformed, going from ovoid to trim. Going from energyless lackluster days to a jones for life once more.

All articles mentioned in passing here are linked to in the Additional Resources segment at the end of this bookito.

One website I came across — WalkAtHome.com — showcases women who've lost significant weight from walking on a treadmill. This site emphasizes walking at home so weather and or other environmental factors don't get in the way of a daily program.

As on many physical transformation sites, the women showcase their before and after photos:

- 45 pounds lost in 12 months
- 25 pounds in 8 months
- 44 pounds in 6 months
- 101 pounds in 30 months

From Prevention.com there's a Walk Your Butt Off page highlighting several similar walking weight-loss stories.

"My Biggest Payoff: *When I look in the mirror, I no longer see an old, fat woman. I see one happy chick!"*

This from a woman who was staring down pre-diabetes at 60 from a lifetime of donuts and ice cream.

Another impressive story concerned a woman who professed not to be a morning person. She managed to keep a walking program going by committing to walking in the evenings, despite a day of work then cooking dinner for her family. Sometimes she didn't get out till after 9 pm. That's heroic in my world, where any drive I have has dissipated fully by the evening hours.

Getting off blood pressure pills, eliminating cholesterol-lowering drugs, ditching meds for a variety of physical and mental ailments — all are by-products of walking and weight loss.

Walking programs and a change in diet go hand in hand. It often happens so effortlessly you barely notice.

I can attest to this in my own life. Once I began my daily walking routine, almost imperceptibly at first, I began to eat better. Something about exercise sparks a desire for healthier eats. Now, years into my walking habit, leaner, feeling more ecstatically alive, my diet has shifted away from meat and processed carbs (like cereals) toward a more nutritional plant-based diet. Gradually. Surprisingly. Easily.

As my physical fitness improved my yearning for junk foods diminished. A similar process happened in my youth: Once I started reading books as a pre-teen, comic books were left in the dust. With scarcely a thought about it. I never looked back.

When you enrich your experience, that which diminishes it seems to creep away from you on its own volition.

Spur the body, spark the mind

Not mentioned in the bodily transformation articles is this byproduct: Mental clarity. Were the thrust of the articles different we might have instead heard stories of improved recall, sharper responses, greater clarity in their day-to-day activities. With only a little prompting these individuals would have noted with some surprise a new relationship between thought and will power. They undoubtedly felt more in control of taking action when needed. When a new possibility appears in their now shimmering brain, it will be easier to — ah, sorry — step in that direction.

I know because it happened to me. The sedentary fog lifts when you move more and eat better. Instead of inches you feel as though you can see for miles. In 360 degrees. You not only feel greater clarity as you look forward, you gaze upon your past with a kinder eye. You peep sideways and can now see pathways not taken, ones you could still hop over to if you wish to put in the effort.

As my own walking program ratcheted down my catastrophic health issues, ones that had taken me to the hospital several times with a wildly beating heart, I too gained clarity. In retrospect I shouldn't be surprised that walking 45 minutes to an hour daily coincided with a shift in our fortunes. We were able to sidestep almost certain business death. Had I remained bloated and be-fogged and subpar physically, the mental energy and new strategies needed to reach escape velocity from our situation would likely have eluded us.

Consistent moderate exercise leads to something else unexpected. Cravings for crap foods diminish. Almost effortlessly. It's the eighth wonder of the world. Maybe even the first — you're demoted, Great Pyramid of Giza. Suddenly you find yourself in a virtuous cycle, mobile, vital, craving more of what's good for you, less of what's bad.

These people lost ample weight from walking programs — some over 100 pounds — yet virtually unmentioned was something they gained of equal significance: Clear thinking.

The body is the fastest way to affect the brain, negatively and positively. Overload your body with sugars — we've all felt that fuzzy feeling — and you deaden your most precious resource, your ability to think.

A hundred some odd years ago an American came up with the idea of a vactrain — a train that could be propelled at tremendous speeds in a vacuum tube. A few years later a Russian professor created the first prototype of a workable vactrain. Decades after this the concept was dusted off and refined, adding maglev into the mix. Magnetic levitation. By using magnets to propel the metal body off tracks, the train would suspend eerily in a near-airless tube as it sped forward.

Tesla's Elon Musk resurrected and perfected the idea, renaming it the Hyperloop. With so little resistance from wind and wheels the maglev vactrain could run at hundreds of miles an hour. This is possible because the wall of wind in a partial vacuum tube is removed. Energy lost from wheels grinding on tracks isn't frittered away. The Hyperloop is near frictionless travel.

It is the same with body and mind. The most resistance-free way to affect the mind is through the body. Mind and body are entwined so thoroughly you could call it vacbrain. What moves the body moves the brain. What improves the body improves the brain. And walking is nature's simplest yet most sophisticated vactube.

Honed by hundreds of thousands of years of evolutionary design, walking is nature's near-frictionless path to mental upgrade.

Can we say clear-sighted too?

As with any exercise outdoors, walking naturally exercises the eyes at both mid and far distances. Your eyes are constantly adjusting when you're walking — to the bird swooping above, to the ground in front of you, the buildings to your left and right, the trees, the clouds, the cars, landscaping, colors, passersby.

As I write this I'm near 60 — I strongly suspect all my walking over the years is the reason I can still pass the driver's license eye exam without glasses. And I wore glasses when I was younger!

Nature therapy

I lived in the big bad City for 11 years — New York City — yet every chance I got during a day off I was biking or hiking in Central Park and Riverside Park. Hiking, not walking — because when you carry a backpack filled with frisbee, water, blanket, books, magazines, wallet, sunglasses, snacks, tokens and more — the gear required for navigating the City on a weekend day — it's no mere traipse down the stairs. It's urban hiking, man. You're hefting a substantial weight onto your back and heading into the urban forest.

What's interesting in hindsight is where my friends and I were drawn — to the biggest parks nearby, the ones studded with trees, water, natural earth, grasses, flowers, dog poop.

In a cleverly titled article for *Outside Magazine* — Take Two Hours of Pine Forest and Call Me in the Morning — Florence Williams writes about the Japanese government push to get its citizens out of its cities and into nature. To detox body and spirit from the toxic overwork in Japanese society. They have a term for death by overwork, for God's sake: *Karoshi.*

To their credit Japanese authorities have recognized this problem and are doing what they can to alleviate it. In the article Williams asks her guide:

"What's the Japanese word for stress?" I asked.

"Stress," he said.

They've imported our lifestyle, why not import the word that best defines it?

People in cities who live near large green spaces are less stressed than those farther away. One theory about why walking in nature improves our mood suggests it's due to our hunter-gatherer roots. That great expanse of pre-history when we roamed and foraged and hunted. Walking in nature reduces inflammation. It also increases natural killer cell production — they attack viruses and tumors — which means a casual hike through the woods is cancer fighting.

Walking in nature is a de-stresser. Even in cities you can get in your nature time — or nature bath as the Japanese call it. *Shinrin-yoku* — nature bathing. Just don't go naked as you would when you actually bathe, metaphors only go so far in protecting you from the law.

I can walk into the woods with a problem

and walk out with a solution.

~ German saying

Pole walking

On the physical side, you've come to the segment closest to my rhythmically beating heart, where I advocate for pole walking. Or Nordic walking as some call it. It couldn't be more basic, it's simply walking or hiking with two poles.

Why? For the robust physicality of it. Maybe there's an aspect of protection too, against wild animals and feral humans. Where I live in the rural suburbs of South Florida, we've encountered dogs, snakes, racoons, rabbits, turkeys, an alligator, a wild boar, and sandhill cranes sauntering down the roads. Cranes sound idyllic until you're up close; these creatures are scary tall when you're only a few feet away from them, with a 7-foot wingspan. There's also one particularly malicious small bird constantly harassing the tail feathers of larger birds in the air that has dive bombed me!

You do have to be careful though when you launch into self-defense mode with your poles. I almost took myself out once flapping the poles wildly around my head to ward off a horsefly.

Here's one thing I can guarantee: No one's going to mug you armed with two poles. They'll move on to easier prey.

Soooooo, that was a digression — and not at all what this segment is about:

When you walk with two poles you engage your upper body far more vigorously than otherwise. You'd be surprised how much the seemingly slight weight of your poles turns into a healthy upper-body ache the longer you go. Plus, for the calorie conscious, you burn an additional 20% to 40% in calories.

When I've pole walked with friends unaccustomed to poles, they can get winded — even ones who are in otherwise decent shape. Especially if we're going a distance. The extra weight along with the natural swing of your arms as you move with the poles gives you an additional workout. Which adds to the aerobic load as you walk.

To strength train while walking — particularly for upper body and torso fitness — is a twofer you shouldn't pass up.

Seriously, please consider this for yourself. This is my second most earnest entreaty in this bookito besides daily walks themselves. By adding poles you turn your walks into full-body workouts.

I've gone a tad overboard with my poles. I love loping down the dirt roads in our area with cut tree limbs for walking sticks. In South Florida the Brazilian Pepper is an invasive tree species choking out native flora, and the fauna that lives from it. It looks like an overly large bush from a distance, growing as wide as it is tall. (About 3o feet.) (For those of you quick at math, that's four sandhill cranes running at you wingtip to wingtip.) Because it crowds out native species, the state recommends eradication wherever possible — and I do my part! —

manually. Every year I battle with these invaders mano a mano.

The Brazilian Pepper grows fast. For my purposes it also has one exquisite feature — the limbs shoot out straight and far as it lasers through other foliage seeking light, making for ideal walking poles when cut to proper lengths.

These cut limbs are of varying diameters and lengths. I must have 20 of them leaning against our house to choose from for a walk; the longer the excursion the leaner the poles I'll choose. On short hikes when I want a heavier load, I select the bigguns.

My teenage son and his friends love using them for sword battles — and for whacking against trees. They're not happy till the poles are cracked in two and splintered. Luckily for me — ? — the Brazilian Pepper is always shooting up fast somewhere on our property, supplying me with replacements.

Because these natural walking poles are heavier than the manufactured variety, I can get in much more of a workout, depending upon the girth and weight I choose for a particular walk.

A side benefit of walking poles: You can use them as you would weights, alternately pumping one then the other up in the air — repeatedly. Till you're winded.

I also like extending my arms straight out to the sides of my body as I walk, raising the poles high above my head till they meet, then easing them back down to shoulder level. Like a cheerleader with pom poms. Up down up down up down up down …

You do this enough times and you'll feel the burn. With a little creativity you'll find variations of upper body strengthening to employ for short intervals as you walk. Once you hit your limit with any particular sequence, dropping back into regular walking mode with the poles feels like sweet relief.

There are other ways to make your walks more physically demanding too. If you're wanting to work out your musculoskeletal system even more, two of the easiest are ankle weights and weight vests.

In this time of coronavirus as this bookito darts to publication, some sexy celebs have been spotted out for walks wearing ankle weights. The better to tone those bods even more. Ankle weights act like a bracelet, resting just above the foot. They are soft, low weight and comfortable, fastening with velcro or pull straps.

I didn't even know weight vests existed until a couple summers ago when we hiked to the peak of Mount Erie in Washington. At the top, taking in expansive views of the coastline, the Pacific, islands a James Bond villain would covet — oh, and Canada — our party of four — me, Ann, our teenage son Zane and his friend Wes — was surprised by a studly young dude who came running up behind us, barely winded. He was training for a grueling mountain-terrain marathon. As we marveled that he'd just run the very trails we'd labored up to summit this mountain, he casually pointed to the sleek chic sportvest he was wearing over his shirt — a weighted vest! — to add intensity to his workout.

Yeah, so you can do that too. Add ankle cuffs and a weight vest to your walks — your pole walks — for the ultimate body workout.

Leaner more muscular you beckons to current you. Slightly future you implores, *Take up pole walking!* Listen to more optimal you — you only want the best for you.

Important to note — you don't need to cut tree limbs as some crazies are wont to do. You can buy adjustable aluminum walking poles online with the merest of searches. Search for walking poles, trekking poles, hiking poles or Nordic poles.

My ideal manufactured pole would allow for slender metal tubes to be slid down the length to add weight when wanted. I've not seen these out in the marketplace … perhaps some intrepid reader will take up that challenge, eh?

A trend on the rise?

We've lived in our neighborhood for seven or eight years. When I first began walking with poles I was alone. I was the lone oddity getting an upper body workout while out for a stroll. Everyone else walked or ran or cycled the way people always do. In the last year though I've seen 3 or 4 guys using walking poles.

All it takes is one eccentric to get a trend started.

A pole walking story (cleverly foreshadowing the next theme)

Just today I was out pole walking in my neighborhood. Dirt roads spring off our paved street like teeth off a comb. For this walk of only 25 minutes I had the Ground Thumpers with me. They're damn near tree stumps. A tracker with an ear to the ground would swear a pachyderm was nigh.

On my favorite jaunts the vegetation is South Florida dense, tropical and lush. Vines grow on trees springing up through palmettos lording it over grasses and scrub brush. Each home is a rural delight. Highly individuated, idiosyncratic even. Well, not every home, every now and then someone has clearcut the land and you wonder, *What the bloody hell?! Why didn't you stay in the suburbs?*

Of course it's exactly the ones who clearcut the land you never see outdoors. It's not like they're rolling around in the grass or frisbeeing it up.

No, they're the ones who clear the land because they can, leaving a gaping garish flat fart of a landscape in their wake. The earth cries and I cry with it.

As I strode by, a happy white beast of a dog trotted over. It immediately and playfully rounded me, stepping to my front to thwart my progress, and proceeded to sniff spoor from my own dogs like he was reading the hometown news.

His owner, a hale fellow not far behind, introduced himself. We'd long admired the horses in a corral to one side of his property. With scarcely half a sentence of appreciation for his landscaping as a prompt, Brent drew me in for a tour du plantlife. From ginger to pineapple to South American cherry tree to Georgia peach tree to lemon to avocado to grapefruit to tomato plants we went.

Turns out he's in the lumber harvesting business — the *underwater* lumber harvesting business in Central and South America. Who knew there was such a thing? As Brent said, it was evolutionary. His family didn't start out farming underwater, they began with traditional lumber. You entrepreneurial types know how that goes. You're doing standard tree farming and you extract some semi-submerged logs along the shoreline sent down river in a previous generation. When you find out there's a market for this type of lumber, step by step you go deeper into the water, until one day the submerged foresting operation is your primary business.

One of the wood types Brent's company specializes in is *ipe*, a hard wood apparently made even more durable from years underwater. Pronounced ee-pay, ipe is ideal for outdoor decking. It can easily last a hundred years with minimal maintenance. Like I personally want to do — last a century with only the faintest bit of upkeep.

They do two types of underwater farming for ipe, both fascinating. In times past the logging industry sent the timber bundled together down river. Those ipe tree bundles that burst apart,

sank. The wood is that dense. So Brent and people like him use sonar and other sounding
methods to locate this sunken treasure — then
retrieve it.

A second method is to go where rivers have
been dammed up. The valley bowls formed
lakes warehousing thousands upon thousands of
dead trees, still standing sentinel eerily from the
now lake bottom. With air tubes driven by
compressors atop a barge, divers descend to cut
down (cut up?) these long-drowned trees.

There are a few other ways I might have come
across this information. All of them involved
sitting on spreading buttocks, say watching a reality show or documentary on the subject, or
maybe internet hopscotching, leaping from link
to link to link until a fortuitous path brought
me to an article about this very process. Underwater tree farming.

But look what walking wrought! Brent must be
the warmest-hearted human on the planet. His
voice is engaging. He exudes warmth. And he
had noticed me striding by his home with

makeshift poles on more than one occasion … I'm over 5 decades old and none of the sitting methods brought me to this subject. It was chance. Chance aided by pedestrianism.

Walkers — those without sound in their ears — invite dialogue. And if you're lucky, friendship.

If you set out with an open spirit, you'll connect with others along the way. Not always. Not everyday. But often enough to enlarge your domain. All it takes is a hello … and being open to those who want to engage you.

WALKING AS CONNECTION

Within and without

Jesus walked. From town to town. Drawing in devotees and the curious in his travels, to hear his message of good tidings. An itinerant rabbi of uncommon charisma, Jesus piqued interest on roads and in village after village — *by walking there*. Traveling by foot placed him in proximity to those he sought to influence.

Can you envision a Greek thinker without also imagining him strolling back and forth, teaching, debating, conversing?

Everyone's favorite philosopher — Socrates — walked barefoot daily, discarding even sandals, wearing minimal clothing year round, not feeling warmth or cold he claimed. He was a minimalist 2,400 years before minimalism was cool — there's an early adopter for you.

Though unknown to each other personally because they were born 86 years apart, Aristotle and Socrates were connected through the most common of activities. Socrates walked and talked with young Plato. Plato in turn walked and talked with his student Aristotle.

For nearly a decade and a half Master Kong — Confucius as he is best known to us in the West in this era — traveled with his disciples from kingdom to kingdom, searching for an ideal ruler to whom he could impart his wisdom on governance. They traversed ancient China mostly on foot.

Belly buttons come in two categories, innies and outies. It's the same with connection; there are two modes: Personal and interpersonal. Interior and exterior. The One and the many. In the instances above they overlap. What we know best of Jesus and the Greeks and Confucius came from when they walked and talked with others.

Walking is a means to supreme connection — a ritual for forging treasured relationships or a portal to the profoundest riches of your inner being. We'll explore both in this section. Let's start with connection to others before moving to connection within….

Just walk beside me and be my friend.

~ Albert Camus

Shooteley Ooteley

When I mentioned I was writing a bookito about walking, my sister asked about the themes. I shared the main thrusts: creative thinking, spiritual reflection and body-brain vigor.

I posed a question to myself once — *If there were only one practice you could undertake that would most help you spiritually, creatively and physically ...* before I could even finish the question the answer rushed forward: Walking!

I relayed this to my sister.

Me: "I mean, think of all the issues you can resolve ..."

Charlene: "Yes! Walking is better than counting to 10! Get out of the house — Walk for 10!"

My brother and I, we have one sister, yet she's been saddled with many names. Mostly by me.

Doodle

Boodle Badle Banzer Baby

Carolina Gasolina

Carobina

Charbunkle

Chartreuse

Char dee Char Har dee Har

Char the Star

Char Char

Shoo Shoo

Shooteley Ooteley

And one we'll simply refer to under the acronym BSG to protect her honor

But she's right. Best advice ever for any heated flashpoint:

Get up, get out — walk for 10.

We live far apart, I'm in Florida, she's outside of Chicago. Occasional art trips swing me by her burb. When we get together a favorite activity is to go for a walk at the end of the day.

There's nothing like taking an hour to walk the neighborhood. When you take a walk from someone's front door, the environment naturally nudges conversation in revealing directions. There you are passing a park, a short stretch of the local shopping district, homes of friends, homes of the kids' friends, homes of note, homes of interesting people, homes of odd characters, homes of local infamy ("The guy who lived there defrauded several people in the area in an investment scam. A divorce is underway.")

It's almost standard practice now, for us to grab a walk if we can. Even better if her husband Charlie can come with us. The same principles that make a walk ideal for ideation, make it perfect for bonding. A slowly changing environment at not too arduous a pace sets the mind free. Meaningful if hopscotchy dialog always ensues.

(Get this, this is how cool my sister is — she sends me Charticles! Articles she thinks I'll find intriguing. These are *sooooooo* much better than the clippings my parents sent when I left home … I actually look forward to reading them. Not that I didn't appreciate passages on how best to avoid constipation, Mom. Char sends articles about architectural trends in Chicago; how innovation is sparked by *adjacent possibilities* — the least I can do is dream up endless pet names for her.)

(*Shoo Fly*)

(*Shooby Wooby*)

(*CharShank Redemption*)

Friends and lovers

You've often heard me suggest, *Walk without sound in your ears.* To that I add an exclamation point — ! — for emphasis. The greatest benefits of a solitary walk accrue to those who sally forth with nothing but ambient sound to accompany their thoughts. Yet to every rule there's an exception. My exception to this directive is the sound of friends and lovers. Bring them along if you can! Even if you must port them through your phone while striding sidewalks and pathways.

I oftentimes take a friend or family member on a walk, one who is miles away — hundreds even thousands of miles away.

A favorite friend is a walker. He's one of the first I called when embarking on this project. To get his take, to ask *why he walked?* He's the walkiest person I know. *What does walking mean to him?* He and I have enjoyed walks since our college days, roaming the streets of

Winter Park, Florida, into the late-night hours. This enjoyment for moving while communing followed us wherever we went, from college, to our later New York City days to Southeast Florida where we both reside now. When we get together it is almost always for a walk.

We've talked dreams. For the near future, for the nebulous distant future. We've talked women. We've talked frustrations. The latter two are not necessarily linked, though they're not necessarily unlinked either. We've talked philosophy — the real kind, why we do what we do. We've talked *what the hell do I do now* at many a crossroad. We've talked inspiration. We've talked thwarted ambitions. We've talked momentum.

Gil responded to my email by leaving two rambling-ish messages, because that is his way. Below I've edited out the extraneous — because some sentences looked like this: "Yeah, it's god— I don't— It's ahh, I don't know, it goes beyond words what it means to me, and I don't, you know, there's some things I can think of off the top of my head but it's really, it's an understatement, I don't know, it's just, I have a bias against people in construction, it's the environmental thing, I didn't say—"

At that point he interrupted himself again and hopscotched over to thoughts on running.

Besides rapidly-firing synapses, do you want to know why Gil ended up all over the place while he was leaving messages about how much walking meant to him? Because he was *walking*! He was moving. Visual details intruded into his train of thought. Sounds and cars and passersby hopped onboard as well. He was walking at the threshold between suburb and shopping district. A lot was happening around him and he was responding to it. It wasn't an express train, his thought stream, his was a local that hit every stop — and then made unscheduled detours as well.

Here's the slightly edited Gil:

It's so many different things. It's a de-stressor. It's a clearing of the mind. Or when I listen to something, an enrichment of the mind. It's some exercise, that's the least of it. Sometimes it's the only part of the day I really enjoy. It's an escape. Personal time.

It does mean a lot. I go through so many different phases because I do so many different things. Sometimes I walk in silence. Sometimes I make a phone call. Lately I've been listening to podcasts. Sometimes I'll do many different things during that time. I'll journal. I'll make calls. Sometimes I'll listen to music, I just want to zone out. So just some free time. And I'm in motion ... the times when you are silent I'm communing with nature, it's a beautiful walk, I'm taking in the trees, the water, the gator I just saw.

What else? And it's—

I'll say this about the walking, it's all I can do now. I mean I can swim. The point I'm trying to make is it's not merely ... I hate to use the word spiritual, but I can't think of a different word.

From just one man's experience with his daily walks you get a sense of the kaleidoscope of meaning walking can have for a committed walker. Those of us who walk fumble for its meaning, though ultimately — even for the nonreligious, nonbelievers, non-likely to ascribe greater meaning to common experience — we all seem to find our way to *spiritual*. Walking has a spiritual component to it that can't be measured or broken down or dissected. It grounds and connects.

Inflection points

One night in New York City a forever friend and I ended up walking back from the bars and restaurants to my place. Russell was visiting from Florida, where he was visibly destroying himself. To the casual observer it might have seemed lifestyle issues were taking their toll — the excesses of drink and drug. To a friend it seemed something deeper, an internal rift. Raised a conservative Christian, Southern Black, son of the South and son of a military man — none of these allowed for gay.

I'd worked till late, catching up with Russell after his evening out with college theater friends. Foreshadowing a walking ritual we would re-enact many times in the future, we walked from the upper reaches of the Upper West Side back to Hell's Kitchen where I lived, where our friend Gil lived.

The after-midnight walk hadn't burned off the alcohol, not nearly. Once we turned onto 46th

Street Russell crumpled onto brownstone steps, anguishing over the burning contradictions in his life.

He couldn't reconcile his same sex attraction with family and religion. Others are able to cast off the religion of their youth, the one that doesn't align with who they've become, not Russell. He's always been a man of faith — couldn't do that. On those steps he bewailed that his God condemned his inclination, that his parents would reject him were they to discover his orientation. It was tearing him apart. You could hear it in his voice, ragged and raw from the war within.

It seemed the legacy of his upbringing was killing him. Still visibly affected by the consumption of the night, Russell was by turns bitter, agonized, defeated, his voice cracking.

I'd left the South that entombed him, but it wasn't the South of Russell's 1960s' North Carolina upbringing. Mine had been the South of coastal Florida, where influxes of engineers and businessmen and laborers and retirees from around the country wove a broader viewpoint into our community. NASA was so close we watched rockets escape earth from our backyards. I'd emerged from the New South, he'd come of age in the Deep South.

Russell's desolation compelled my counter narrative — just as urgently I pleaded with him to move to New York City, where it was OK to be Black and gay and Christian. Southern even.

Dutiful beloved last son of five, the baby wunderkind who'd done the family proud by becoming the first to blast his way through graduate school, neither his family position nor his accomplishments offered relief.

He'd only ever lived in North Carolina and Florida. Orlando of the 1980s held little benefit for one who could scarcely breathe a breath of his own individuality for fear of reprisal.

I argued for a move. *Sometimes you simply need to move to a place that welcomes you.*

Russell had gone to law school, not to become a lawyer, for his parents. So much of his life had been lived conforming contorting comporting to external demands. In epigenetics it is the environment external to the cell that induces changes in genetic expression. For Russell, it had been an epi-life to that point, living according to the dictates of those around him.

His soul was riven — the walk and the alcohol and the City had loosened his constraints. You could see it all coming out. Gil must have been working — we were freelancers then, keeping odd hours. It was just Russell and me and his heartbreak.

God didn't want his kind — it was wrong — he lusted after men — his mother who loved him dearly thought gayness abominable — his military father would have seen it as weakness, aberration.

There was no place for him.

Yes there is, I said — *it's here. Here it's OK to be gay and Godly.*

Here it was OK to be black and gay and sensitive.

Move to New York was my refrain.

Move to New York, I repeated. It became a kind of call and response as Russell poured out his torment.

Move or your going to die—

He did.

He moved to the City. Russell went on to an accomplished career. He went on to integrate his sexuality and his spirituality, even singing for years in a choir in the church positive thinker Norman Vincent Peale once helmed.

Later this forever friend demonstrated how to take care of a distant but dying father. By stepping up and doing what duty demanded. By doing one's duty no matter how nasty. Russell's example glowed as a kind of beacon with my own father a few years after. In his case, he showered his doddering father, a man sometimes spattered with his own waste. He clipped his nails. He shaved him. He undressed him and cleaned him, driving several hours back home each weekend to fulfill his duty.

Not long ago Russell unexpectedly became the caretaker and ward for a friend he'd only known in his youth a few years. As an adult with cancer she reached out to Russell because they lived in the same city. Not even especially close to her in childhood, by degrees he became her aide and confidante, protector and lackey. She was demanding! The cancer freed her from inhibitions in making requests of others. If indeed she'd had any — perhaps why her family stayed away.

That's Russell, a man who values his solitude, who will drop everything for you when called by circumstance.

During the crash years when I was a nomad roaming the country in a van to save our business, I slept many a night on the road in Russell's apartment each time I drove through his area. Never once did he complain; he saved me hundreds if not thousands in hotel bills. Crucially, Russell was the inflection point in many a trip, psychologically and physically. Every time we met up our ritual was to go for a walk.

Soul schisms can sometimes be solved by walking. Not all at once, not even all of them every time. Yet — it's true — with a friend — or alone — or communing with your spiritual source — walking can lead to transformation — in the subtlest of ways — in an inflection point — one that changes what you think possible. And thus changes your trajectory oh so slightly, enough to change your path.

Russell and I have done that for each other throughout the years.

This lifelong friend now lives in Charlotte, North Carolina. Our thing is to walk the local cemetery. It's not a somber experience, we joke with the dead as we saunter the grounds. Despite its heritage — there's a section honoring Confederate fallen — we lark through this cemetery every day we can — sometimes twice in a day — a Black man and a White man whose friendship spans decades, doing our part to vanquish the ideals of the Confederacy a century and a half later.

Side by side

Though she mocks my hiking poles, my wife Ann is a favorite walking companion. Whenever I can cajole her from her studio we take to the dirt roads nearby, visiting goats, chickens, or a grand old turkey en route.

We pass hundreds of flourishing friendly trees, trees of every tropical variety. Little is superior to ambling through nature with one you love, chit chatting about the mundane and the lofty.

Walk with a friend or lover and it's inevitable you'll deepen your bond.

Special time with pets

Kate VanNoorden, in her mid-80s, is an animal sculptor of some fame I'm honored to call friend. She too is an avid walker, venturing outside several times a day with her dogs and the dogs she boards. Here are some of her thoughts on walking with pets:

Walking — Mostly with dogs so it's really more of a sniff n pee, more like someone reading the newspaper. Sometimes so slow I accuse my Great Pyrenees of being bogged down in pages about the stock market.

During this time — their time — I don't use my cell phone. It is THEIR time and I want to be with them mentally as well as physically. BUT this amble — yes, mostly it qualifies as an "amble" — makes for quality observation time of the small stuff in the world around me.

I love the small stuff, like the tiny periwinkle blue flower that grows in the grass along our walk at the park, or the lovely white "Florida

Frost." How can it continue to blossom after days of being trampled?

Its purpose I think must be in telling us to look down at the beauty at our feet. Classified as weeds — something we have determined is growing in the wrong place — some of the loveliest flowering things are scorned and mostly hauled out with nary a nod to their variety and perfection.

Kate enjoys how slow walking with her dogs allows her to sift through the issues swirling in her head. More than this, she seeks to *pray without ceasing* when on a walk — a Biblical injunction to rejoice perpetually, to give thanks in all circumstances. Kate wants to allow herself to be caught up in the wondrous experience of being out in the world.

I suspect her frequent walks are one of the reasons she's alert, twinkly-eyed and physically capable at an age when so many Americans are tottering in the wreckage of their once-upon-a-time wonderful bodies.

I understood at a very early age that in nature,
I felt everything I should feel in church
but never did.
Walking in the woods,
I felt in touch with the universe
and with the spirit of the universe.

~ Alice Walker

You become the drug you seek

There are well-trod walking paths in sacred places around this globe, where in contemplation an initiate takes an issue into their heart and walks it out. In my own life when I was in the greatest turmoil mentally – and the greatest bodily deterioration – I embarked on a walking program that long days and mounting debts couldn't deter.

While walking I set different intentions. Sometimes I'd work to find the good in the collapsing business. As anyone who has practiced gratitude knows, it's only work initially. After strained attempts at finding the good in your bleak existence you enter a state of flow where one thing after another trips from your mind – *Damn, those olives were succulent! An Incan emperor couldn't have enjoyed those. Plumbing! I live for that warm, modulated waterfall called a shower — something Charlemagne himself couldn't attain with all*

*his power. The day was transcendently sweet,
wasn't it, if I take away my worries. Oh look at
that squirrel, those kids with their playful ban-
ter, remember when Kelly said something that
made me snort through my nose, oh yeah, and
what about that toilet topic inducing the deli
man to giggle* ... all the goodness tumbles upon
you. There is so much good you can find in a
walk. Your very blood, pumping more heartily,
hastens the process.

Sometimes the intention was mantric — a cir-
cularity of external motion and internal
repetition that invites in the throb of the universe.

Sometimes it was absorption in sensation:
breath becomes thunder; muscles spring and release cat-like; Florida vapors, sweat tingles, loose
fabric, night sounds storm the brain stem — a
bird suddenly takes flight from a tree in the
darkness, leaving us both startled.

There is enchantment and reverie in a solitary
walk.

Many a practice when combined with walking induces a mind-and-spirit melding … You can practice love. You can recite mantras or scripture or affirmations. You can speak declarations aloud — and pretend you were speaking on your cell phone when caught unexpectedly.

There are articles and books and Internet blogs on the subject, on ways to deepen your walking experience. At its core – you in silent motion with your thoughts – there is nothing else you need to know. Your own fine being will articulate its needs.

You can do urban hiking, suburban jaunts, rural ramblings … most anywhere is feasible. Really, where can you not walk?!

One could write a book on the revelations that come one's way solely while walking. Everyone could. And it would be interesting! I promise you. Each and every one.

When you set out on a walk with profound intent, you can recode your brain to your specifications.

Best of all, walking is the opening act to all those other physical activities you aspire to. Soon you're working out, biking, kayaking again, doing Pilates from ceiling straps, having Cirque Du Soleil sex. All those endorphinic moments that send you cresting to new highs when you walk impel you to more activity, more moments of crescendo. That's a virtuous biofeedback loop, baby.

Rain walking

A friend of mine — Mike Cohen — loves walking in the rain. As does my friend Gil. If there's no lightning about.

Why?

Because the drumbeat of raindrops.

Because the waterfall effects of rainshower.

Because the tingle of mist and droplets.

Because it's an immersive experience, one that takes you out of your humdrum thoughts and puts you fully in the moment.

Because it's nature cleansing.

Sometimes a hike is not just a hike

Sometimes a hike is not just a hike, sometimes a hike is an *energy* amplifier. If you yourself have stumbled into the mystic in your meanderings, you know what I mean.

We drove into northern Arizona determined to hike one of the four famous vortexes there. Spiritually attuned individuals have long claimed Sedona has a special energy — in fact that spiritual-energy vortexes lie in four distinct locations around the greater Sedona area. (Though *vortices* is the correct plural, *vortexes* is the plural most commonly used by locals, seekers, shamans, hikers and healers. Newbies like me, too.)

According to lore — and a bevy of websites on the matter — a vortex is a spiraling movement of energy, much like an invisible funnel cloud. One with great if subtle power. Apparently those who are sensitive to it can feel the shift as they approach. It washes over you. You feel radiant. You may even feel incalculable connection to the earth and the cosmos and all that is.

Or maybe not, maybe you simply feel awe for the beauty of the red rock you cling to thrusting hundredsands of feet skyward.

When earlier in the year Ann told me our friend Carolyn had hiked a Vortex and felt something profound, I was all in. Since I believe in everything, I was game.

The scientist and the mystic

Carolyn Cohen is one half of a paradoxical couple who are great friends of ours. When I first met them I was struck that I'd never met two people — two people joined together in a marriage — who spoke such different languages. Mike spoke science while Carolyn spoke energy. As in New Age energy. Spiritual energy.

Mike is a grounded, highly cerebral neurofeedback practitioner. (Biofeedback for the brain — healing brain-related issues without drugs: Anxiety, depression, insomnia, hyperactivity/

attention deficit issues and more.) Carolyn is an energy healer with uncanny powers of insight.

Here's an example. When Ann and Carolyn first met, upon finding out what Carolyn did — energy healing — Ann decided to try a session. She was feeling blocked creatively and thought, *Why not, can't hurt.* What transpired was hoodoo of the highest level.

Carolyn, who knew little about Ann at the time, proceeded to lightheartedly mimic Ann's parents to an eerie degree in their first session. As she called on the energies of Ann's parents, Carolyn portrayed their behavior *as it was in real life* — Ann's Dad taking an interest, followed immediately by Ann's Mom rushing in, drawing him back to her own orbit. Ann's Mom had always been a chaotic and controlling figure, actively discouraging communication between Ann and her father — and Carolyn, with no knowledge of them or their dynamic, nailed it *exactly*.

Hence our nicknames for them: The scientist and the mystic.

We parked the MoFave — Mobile Ops Family Adventure Vehicle — a sparkling gunmetal grey van to the rest of humanity — in a parking lot within sight of Bell Rock. At first we hiked through southwestern scrub along flat pathways, crunching and scuffing our way through the high desert.

Then came the red rock outcroppings. At first you clamber up gentle sloping rock inclines — the skirts of Bell Rock, so to speak. Bell Rock, unsurprisingly shaped like a bell if a bell were ridged, allows for climbers of all aptitudes to mount some bit of it. The lowest reaches can be gotten by almost anyone who's ambulatory. As you rise up, each new ridge level attained winnows out more of the hikers. Because each ridge extends widely — hundreds of feet horizontally — each hiker or group can find an easy perch that almost feels like solitude. You just wander to the left or the right of the main pathways and before long you'll discover a nook, a boulder, a groove in the rock, a worn wall or niche, the perfect spot for you to plunk down and grok the vibe. Bell Rock is unforgettable — rich saturations of red and ochre at the mid level, a yellowy stone atop, patchy greens on the desert floor between the upjutting mountains nearby.

Our son Zane, twelve at the time and a natural-born clamberer, sped far beyond us, far higher, till we had to yell for him to stop. If we hadn't he might still be climbing upward today....

Ann found a spot for herself. Minutes later I found mine. We intended to intend! To get quiet — and to feel the place. To feel the enormity and the antiquity of it — the startling aliveness of it — until at some point you realize you feel it within you too, quite apart from your surroundings.

You too feel eternal and special and significant even as you also feel weirdly transient, temporary. Yet it's not off-putting. The rock and you are here now for a short while. Zoom out far enough in deep time and you and the rock are gone. Does it really matter if one is a human lifetime and the other runs through lifetimes of multiple species, long forgotten?

(272 million years, that's the age of Bell Rock, so you don't have to look it up.)

It's all a blip — and it's all the eternal present. The rock is grounded and so are you. The rock is hard and dense though we know from physics 99.9% of it is empty space. You are soft though durable enough, and also mostly empty space. The rock is still and wise and so are you. The rock is enigmatic, so are you! The rock is beautiful and so are you.

You may have questions for science — *How did this area form? Why the predominance of reds? Who first settled here? Why so little growth in the upper reaches?* — but those are for later. Here, now, in your forever moment, while you are affixed to Bell Rock, the mystic reigns.

Drop it on the trail

Eleven months after a near-fatal illness, Chandi Wyant returned to the one country she felt deeply connected to — Italy — to embark on a pilgrimage of healing. Despite her enfeebled condition, she hiked the Via Francigena, an ancient trail over mountains, through Tuscany, eventually into the heart of Rome. In her book *A Return To Glow* she writes about how she felt upended by her health issues, the disintegration of her marriage.

Along the trail, many miles into her journey, an epiphany surfaces:

Spontaneously, a message comes to me: Drop along the trail the weights of the past in order to receive the gifts of today. It becomes a mantra that stays with me as I continue on the leafy lane. I start to name the weights and metaphorically drop them as I walk.

My list, said aloud and witnessed by the oak trees, goes like this:

"My divorce. Okay, but what about my divorce? The idea that I'm flawed because I got a divorce. Do I have that idea? Okay, drop it on the trail anyway.

"The idea that it's stuck in my body. Yes, that's a good one. Drop it on the trail!"

I start to swing my trekking poles and point them at the weights I drop, which I picture as plate-sized dung heaps.

"Umm ... what about ... how I choose the wrong guys? Let's drop that too, and Mutton Head. Good riddance!"

I stride on, down the car-less lane.

"I'm dropping the idea that I shouldn't be in my power."

"I'm dropping the fear of speaking my truth."

Why do we do that? Play small?

"Drop it on the trail!"

We could all live lives more filled with wonder if we dropped our baggage on the trail. I don't mean upending careers and families to strike out for weeks on end in a faraway land, nay, no, of course not — I mean simply making it a practice to unstrap our burdens and drop them during a regular walk.

Something weighing you down? Drop it on the trail! Drop it beside the sidewalk. Drop it in a yard. We're excluding pet waste here — or anything tangible, really, we want to be neighborly. Whatever plagues you, drop it.

Drop it, stop it, lop it off, that psychic disturbance you're carrying. There's no better place than on a walk.

The labyrinth of Ojo Caliente

Ojo Caliente is a natural hot spring in northern New Mexico fabled for its healing power. As you enter the courtyard where the baths and pools are situated, you encounter a walking labyrinth.

It's instantly calming once you set foot inside. The labyrinth is but a simple spiral on the ground— a lane lined with hand-placed stones to mark its curves. You step into the outermost opening, following the path as it curls toward the center. The act of walking deliberately, slowly, eyes down, induces an almost somnambulistic state. At the axis point lie a small pile of stones. You get the feeling some of the walkers might have held these rocks as meditative touchstones as they walked lazily inward — and placed them there as an offering of sorts.

Once you reach the center you pause, give a blessing, ask for a transformation for yourself or someone else, set an intention, or steep in that pivot point between entering and departing…. Then you step forward, and find yourself un-spooling outward, magically released back into the courtyard you never left.

When I arrived at the center point I gave thanks, for all that is right in my world — there was more good and right in it than I could begin to consciously acknowledge. Like the mineral spring itself, once you tap that vein it flows and flows—

Walking as meditation

Walking is the only meditation many will get. Avail yourself of this gift!

When you walk without sound in your ears an entrainment of mind, soul and body is inevitable. You can't help but become aligned. Like Chandi Wyant on the Via Francigena, you feel you can drop psychological weights anywhere along your route. Issues have a way of working themselves out. Resolutions pop to mind. Ways to solve a problem bubble up from your be-calmed brain.

Once you've set out for a walk without distractions, it's not long before you tune into the space you're moving through. You become attentive to small things. The sound of a squirrel scrapping its way up pine bark. Wind through foliage. Car colors. Bumper stickers. The sound of your poles thudding the ground. Open sky. Cloud formations. All the variants of green if you're in the East. Clay or rock if you're in the Southwest. The cacophony of the city if you're in any urban anywhere.

You sync with your surroundings. When you walk without the distraction of sound you merge with the environment. You pick up cues. The barrier between you and everything else melts. Psychologically you become attuned. The worlds within and without spin in the same direction. You feel you could dip a paddle into the stream of reality and glide to a new trajectory.

Contemplative walking: The issue evaporator

Contemporary spirituality emphasizes stillness — mindfulness — being in the moment — sometimes to the detriment of a method that has served humans for millennia: Contemplative thought. Which is simply to think about one question at length until the issue resolves itself.

Just as in a creation walk, an *issue walk* or a *contemplative walk* is all about letting your mind slip in and around a focal point from multiple angles.

They're twins really — the creation walk and the contemplative walk — with different temperaments. One is about something you wish to create, the other is about something you wish to resolve. It's easy to see how they overlap.

A contemplative focuses on one issue — one question, one theme — looking at it from myriad viewpoints, and by doing so gains greater understanding. Exploring one line of thought with gentle persistence will yield answers.

A contemplative walk is the easiest mode in the world. Most of us do it naturally in other contexts. We set out in our car and find ourselves obsessing over something vexing us. The ride and its thrum of motor and motion often draws out unconsidered possibilities. We jump in the shower aggravated by someone in our life — and in the course of the shower we find ourselves softening, finding solutions, or happening upon the exact course of action we want to take, becoming resolute when minutes earlier we were floundering.

On a contemplative walk you simply take an issue into your heart and set out.

When you walk without distraction — without talking, without music, without sound in your ears — your mind clears. You enter a dreamy slipstream that pulls you forward, into a fertile state. Curve around an issue long enough, ideas will burble up.

If you have an issue plaguing you, try it: Take it with you, walk it out.

See if you don't feel closer to a resolution after a twenty-minute walk.

If ambitious, go for an hour walk ... do you even have an issue now?

Mini-walkabout

When I lived in Australia for a semester in my final year of college I became enamored with *walkabout.* The term referred to the rite of passage a young Aboriginal Australian male would undertake alone, usually between the ages of 10 and 16. The young aborigine would strike out on his own, fending for himself in the Australian bush, returning months later.

It's not exclusively a coming of age thing. Walkabouts can be undertaken in adulthood also — one simply ventures off. One day they'd be on the job, the next day they'd be off on walkabout.

There's a spiritual connotation to a wandering nomadic adventure. There's a sense of mystery about what might transpire, where the meanderings might lead. No one save the walkabouter really knows. As with any journey only the traveler can inhabit the experience.

The British use the term in a different context. To them *walkabout* tells a different story, that of a person of stature or fame who takes a walk informally among the populace for a short burst, to mingle with the citizenry. As in, *The Queen did a walkabout in Chelsea after lunch.* Or this from a future newspaper clipping, *Beloved bookito author Evan Griffith went walkabout among his fans today at Piccadilly Circus, stopping traffic. The Queen's procession was held up and she was not amused.*

The Brits also have a humorous variation on walkabout — indicating something lost. *My phone has gone walkabout.* Meaning, the phone's gone missing. Note: If your partner goes walkabout, other issues are afoot.

To these three meanings of walkabout I propose a fourth for our modern era. I'd like to repurpose this term for Westerners in particular — for people like me. Like everything else we do, the modern walkabout is zippier, truncated, signifying a brief exploration of a new area on foot.

For us it might be a mini-walkabout — alighting on a non-habitual location — a location you don't customarily visit — then going for an explorational walk. Of whatever time frame you can muster!

It might be 20 minutes of ambling. It could be an hour or two. There is no destination other than exploration.

Here I am on a day off passing a park on the way to an errand. Why not pull over and enjoy a mini-walkabout? Take 20 minutes to walk the pathways. Or it could be in a nearby neighborhood — a shopping zone you have to stop by — a downtown — a beach — anywhere. You hop out of your daily routine to go on a mini-walkabout. Your brief Americanized walkabout. Walking, exploring, taking in the sights and sounds, enjoying the experience, rejuvenating your day.

Walking previously unexplored locations without a strategic endpoint other than circling back to where you started is small adventure of the subtlest kind. Your eyes alight on something novel at every turn. Your mind seeks clues from surroundings as to the best way to traverse a meandering route that will ultimately land you back to your launching point.

Embracing the mini-walkabout concept frees you to walk explorationally wherever you alight.

Spirit walks: Prayer, Appreciation and Mantra

So many variations on a walk!

A spirit walk differs from contemplative walking in this way — you actively draw upon a power greater than yourself for others. And for issues beyond your ability to resolve. The process can take many forms, here are just a few.

If you or someone you care for is in crisis, you might simply walk and pray.

If in a mood to attune to the beneficence in your life, you might walk and bask in an ever expanding appreciative glow.

To clear chaotic tension, you might walk and softly speak a mantra in perpetual repetition until you return.

Or simply go quiet, attentive within and without, and feel the presence of something inexplicably vast, unspeakably magnificent. To walk with reverence and awe in quietude is one of the greatest joys I've known. It's a sublime experience, to walk in creation, sensing energies great and coursing and tumultuous and beyond you, sensing unity and rhyme and song pervading the ten trillion things.

To spirit walk is to summon the great Mystery of being into yourself, to gather the Mystery unto you, into you, releasing yourself to all that can't be explained, only experienced. Like this following experience that happened to me....

Spiritual matrix moment

"By walking we move through the world

not just physically,

but also spiritually."

~ Arianna Huffington

I get this. I too have had transcendent experiences while out for a walk. I've experienced episodes where walking became a kind of lazy swim in a matrixed sea of consciousness — moments of solidarity with the cosmos where I've become boundaryless.

I write about one such time in a work in progress titled *The World Is Freaky Beautiful.*

I'm sharing it with you here as well because the experience underscores what Arianna Huffington alludes to in her insight above.

Late one night on a walk I became enthralled by the voluptuousness of trees. Have you ever seen something anew? It was this way that night for trees. I became fond of each trunk as an Indian trainer might become fond of the hide of the elephants in his charge. Suddenly I could see them in acute stereo vision, hyper real – an increasing sense of adoration spilled over with each passing tree.

It became one of those walks where you're not simply exuding some feeble form of gratitude, instead you find yourself besotted *with everything*. You adore this knot, that cleft – leaf upon twig upon creviced limb, you've never seen such beauty! — from emergent waxy green to scabrous bark – you even begin to eke out a warm acceptance of some sticky personality afflicting your days. This keen rapturous appreciation billows outward, far beyond what you can see....

At one point cutting through an alleyway and coming upon a field ringed by densely-packed homes I found myself fluid, electric, instantly aware that all including me was a continuum. It was as if I saw through the eyes of the physicist. All was a particle-ized projection of immense energy. Me and air and tree and house and space were *charged.*

At the same time it was as if I saw through the eyes of an archangel. All was Spiritflow. All was joyful immersion in the Field of Creation. Me and you – if you'd been there – were wisps of Godthought. I sensed the spiritual-physical matrix we inhabit. I grokked it in. I was in it. Everything was. *And I was it.* In the way you might extrapolate the river from a drop of water, I was that drop, I was that river.

Every particle, every pulse was alive. Everything vibrated and, according to its pitch, drew what was consistent and repelled what was inconsistent with itself.

It is said a fish doesn't know there is an ocean. This fish suddenly got it.

Every pilgrimage in the world involves walking

Not quite true. Some involve prostrating yourself on the ground repeatedly. We'll get to that. But the rest do. Even pilgrimages involving travel by plane, train, boat or vehicle to a sacred destination for religious reasons require walking at the endpoint. If Muslim, if devout, if you are financially able, at least once in your lifetime you will travel by modern conveyance to Mecca for the Hajj. Once there you leave motor transport behind to engage in days of walking and prayer and ritual.

Pilgrimage demands walking *for a reason*. Walking in reverence en masse binds participants together in their common purpose. There is also an element of humility, of making oneself worthy of transcendence. The slowness, the sureness, the simplicity of walking prepares you for something deeper. You don't achieve that by simply stepping from your rented Lambo after jetting in from some foreign shore. In *Wanderlust: A History of Walking,* Rebecca Solnit calls it "earning through suffering."

Even as religious context has waned for many in our era, pilgrimage retains its spiritual gravity. Walking for personal transformation continues to grow in popularity:

Hiking the Appalachian Trail. During peak months hikers complain that it's difficult to find the solitude once expected of such a solitary venture.

Hiking the Pacific Crest Trail. Cheryl Strayed did this in her profligate youth, depicting the experience intimately and at times harrowingly in her memoir *Wild.* (Reese Witherspoon starred in a movie of the same name.) It's so popular now long-distance permits are limited to 50 a day at the Southern Terminus in Campo, California, near the Mexican border — to help space out the hikers.

Hiking the Camino de Santiago over the Pyrenees Mountains from France into Spain. More than 200,000 people a year hike all or part of this 485-mile trek to the fabled resting place of St. James in the town of Santiago de Compostela.

Hiking the Char Dham in India, a pilgrimage that takes you to four sacred Hindu sites. A quarter million people a year partake!

Hiking the Inca Trail to Machu Picchu high in the Andes Mountains in Peru. Like the Pacific Crest Trail, the Peruvian government limits the daily numbers so as not to overwhelm the site. A couple hundred tourists a day are scheduled, with up to 300 additional guides, cooks and porters allowed. Pilgrimage with an entourage, you could say.

Hiking the outer kora of Mount Kailash in Tibet. It is claimed humans have been going on pilgrimage to this unique four-faced mountain for 15,000 years. Woah. And — it's forbidden to climb the mountain. To this day it has not been summited — pilgrims instead hike an outer ring a little over 32 miles in circumference, in the rocky high-altitude sub-zero-at-night even-in-the-summer Himalayas. Here you will also encounter *prostrators* who throw themselves to the ground, crawl forward and then do it again — and again — and again — round the base of Mount Kailash. Show offs.

Hiking the Kumano Kodo in Japan. Along with the Camino de Santiago, the Kumano Kodo is the only other pilgrimage path in the world designated as a World Heritage Site by UNESCO. For a thousand years pilgrims have hiked the 750 miles linking three major shrines and a number of smaller worship spaces encountered along the pathways. It has been called *the march of the ants* because of the number of people traversing the Kumano during the most ideal months.

Truth in the woods

The most famous female slave in the United States may have been prompted to escape because she took a walk in the woods.

In her scant spare time as a young slave, Isabella Baumfree would walk into nearby woods to talk with God. Imagine a young unschooled slave woman taking to nature to walk with her Creator. This time in the woods was her only 'free' time, the only taste a slave woman might have with real personal liberty.

Her sojourns — foreshadowing alert! — led Baumfree to craft a shrine from what was at hand in the forest. Baumfree found such solace there she built a temple from undergrowth and downed tree limbs.

Amongst the trees she conversed with the Divine as though she were haggling with an intimate friend. In one powerful experience she felt God forcefully tell her to *walk away* from slavery — and this she did with her baby girl, leaving her other children behind with their father.

On the day of escape Baumfree left early, well before first light to put distance between herself and her master before the household realized she was gone. She hiked 11.5 miles with her 3-month-old daughter that day, down walking paths and roads, trusting God would deliver her to safety. Miles into her walk to freedom, Baumfree recalled a Quaker who lived in a nearby town. Surely he would take her in.

Quakers — The Society of Friends — had been the first organization in the colonies to publicly repudiate slavery in the strongest of terms. Though it's unlikely Baumfree knew this history, she was familiar enough with Quaker disgust for slavery to know this man might help her find refuge.

Years later unschooled Isabella Baumfree plunged into a life of activism, changing her name to Sojourner Truth, becoming one of the great anti-slavery and women's rights advocates of the 19th century. Speaking from her heart, her history and her passionate belief in equal rights for all, this illiterate ex-slave held thousands spellbound with her oratory.

(Search videos for Ain't I A Woman performances to get a sense of Sojourner Truth's powerful message.)

The woman who would become Sojourner Truth took walks in the woods where she conversed with God, who instructed her to leave.

"I did not run off, for I thought that wicked, but I walked off, believing that to be all right."

Peace Pilgrim

Before the 60s were even a patchouli-oiled glimmer in the cultural eyeball, Mildred Norman changed her name. For 28 years Peace Pilgrim walked for global peace, criss crossing America seven times.

How is this for a dramatic beginning to pilgrimage with a purpose? Wearing what became her trademark blue shirt with the words Peace Pilgrim emblazoned in white across her chest, she stepped out in front of the Rose Bowl Parade in California on the First of January, 1953 — then kept walking.

Fifteen years earlier her life changed in a quiet if dramatic manner: In 1938 she spent a night walking and praying in the woods to discover her mission in life.

"A great peace came over me," she said. "I experienced a complete willingness without reservations whatsoever, to give my life to something beyond myself."

She began "living to give, not to get."

"I did not seem to be walking on the Earth… but… every flower, every bush, every tree, seemed to wear a Halo. There was a light emanation around everything and flecks of gold fell like slanted rain through the air."

There's a theme here: Two women from two races living in two different centuries have shown us the way. Want to deepen your experience, possibly even uncover the purpose of your life? Take a walk in the woods, commune with the divine, ask piercing questions with burning intent.

Fourteen years after her night in the woods Mildred Norman became the first woman to hike the entirety of the Appalachian Trail in one season. Befitting a visionary, she had another epiphany while hiking the trail — to dedicate the remainder of her life to walking for peace — walking for world disarmament and peace among all individuals.

Her vow: *To remain a wanderer until mankind has learned the way of peace, walking until given shelter and fasting until given food.*

IF YOU DO
ONLY ONE THING

What is solved by walking?

Life! Life is solved by walking.

(Without sound in your ears.)

(Ohhhh, that can't be stressed enough.)

(Unless you're chatting with a friend.)

(Even then — leave time on your walk to simply be walking.)

(If you want to suppress ideas, if you want to tamp down the inner voice murmuring beneath your everyday consciousness, by all means, don those earplugs and blast sound into your ears. You won't be able to suppress it all, but you'll do a damn good job damming the flow.)

Choosing to walk

Walking for pleasure, walking for brain-body renewal, requires a certain level of civilization. For the vast expanse of history and pre-history humankind walked from necessity. In our era it's optional. Walking is now a choice. One chooses walking against an array of easier alternatives.

You could more easily pick up your digital device and lose yourself there. You could more easily click on the TV. You could hop in your car and head to a friend's — where you might immediately sit and hang out. You could waddle to the refrigerator and wolf down sugar, carbs and every-thing nice.

So much of what we do engages the buttocks in only one way: Sitting. Meeting a friend for a meal. Going to the movies. Taking in a game. An evening at the theater. Or dance recital. Or poetry slam. Or the Blue Man Group.

What commonality is there between a NASCAR race, a monster truck rally, church, class, a book, binge watching a TV series, a TED Talk?

Sitting on your ass to be engaged by others.

Our entertainment is passive. Even our sports events are geared for us human globules to melt into calorie-consuming quasi-comatose states while watching others perform peak athleticism in front of our inert bodies.

These days when you choose walking without sound, you choose something radical. You choose volition. You choose mind-body-spirit unification. You choose individuality over the hive mind.

Yes, this is as true for any other activity that actually requires being active: Running, kayaking, cycling, skateboarding, weight lifting, aerobics, yoga, mountain climbing, hangliding, jump roping, parcours, housework, yardwork, charity work….

One chooses walking against an enticing array of less demanding options. Yet when you do — when you go for a walk — you are choosing participation over passivity.

The best place to walk

There's no one best place to walk, silly. But if you think about it, there are really only three places to walk on this earth:

1. From where you are

The best place, always and forever, is to walk from wherever you find yourself at the moment.

Even in forlorn locations you'd be surprised what you'll find. During my time on the road trying to save our art business when the market crashed, I would set out from miserable hotels at the end of the day. These were always sad affairs, since the cheapest digs were all I could manage. Sometimes they were on busy streets, strewn with refuse. You know, all the modern-era items that get tossed to the side rather than put in a trashcan: broken glass, smashed beer cans, cigarette butts, condoms. Or a stretch of fast food joints and gas stations without a view to recommend. Other times it might be a small cul-de-sac culminating at the hotel, woods or desert all around.

Even so, setting out from these old motels at the end of the day always brought a sense of relief. I was no longer sitting.

Flash forward a decade to this past summer when I was stranded in Klamath Falls, Oregon. We were on a combination art biz/family trip. Our van conched out at Crater Lake, more than 8,000 feet up. The drive up on the inside sliver of a road cut from the edge of the mountain had us gasping at the vistas. And the sheer drop offs inches beyond the far side of the pavement. No guardrail, not so much as an orange cone to wave goodbye to if one sped merrily off the cliff. Not one of us was looking forward to the drive back down on the outside lane.

Luckily — I guess? — we didn't have to. The van freaked out at the top, some kind of electrical mayhem. The alarm went off without even being on. In a parking lot full of sightseers at a transcendently serene mountain setting. Everyone in the van was desperate to shut it down. Lights blinkered on and off. The alarm wailed. The dashboard shot warning icons across our visual bow.

Then nothing. Silence.

Afraid to try to start her back up we hopped out to climb around Crater Lake. Better to give her a rest, we thought. Plus the park would be closing soon. Though we spent a little while gawking at the alien-planet beauty of the lake — a bowl of placid immensity more than 30 miles around, blue enough to compete with Paul Newman's eyes, cold enough to kill a mountain goat in a short time if it fell in — the real joy for two Florida boys was in the snowpacks on descents sloping away from the rim. Our son Zane re-purposed the windshield sunscreen into a flimsy sled, and he and his friend Wes took turns sliding down the packed snow.

After the fun we waited for a tow truck from a town far far away. We rode down that mountain near midnight, all of us packed into the cab, big ole van teetering just behind us on the tow truck platform. The driver had been up since 6 a.m. I tell you this, I've never sparkled more as a conversationalist, asking questions, recounting road stories, exploring the deep crevices of his life, anything to keep him awake —

The next day my wife rented a car and shot back up into the mountains with the boys while I waited on the van repairs.

The Klamath Falls neighborhood I walked was surreally interesting for its squalor and intrigue. I'd been reading of the opioid epidemic rampant through the U.S. — this area felt like ground zero for this scourge. Some homes had plastic sheeting for windows. Others had boards nailed across the openings, still others the glass remained, cracked, chipped, taped.

What stood out were the homes made tidy, made happy with flower beds, the ones that were painted, the ones standing fiercely against the decay. They were few, though maybe they were the harbingers of change. The wayshowers...

My point is — by simply walking from where I was that day, I witnessed community disintegration — and hints of possible resurrection —

in such a vivid manner the problem of ur-
ban/suburban decay became real to me.

2. At the closest nearby

Nearby there are trails to be hiked.

Nearby there are malls to be walked when heat,
chill or showers prevent it otherwise.

Nearby there are neighborhoods with sidewalks.

Nearby there are downtown walking districts.

Nearby there are parks and fields and options
for the walking.

You just need to get yourself there.

3. Impossibly interesting places

Once while Ann and I were on an art trek we
met up with my brother's family at Chimney
Rock at the edge of the Blue Ridge Mountains
in North Carolina. Both families were traveling
through the South — Ann and I on our way to
the art scene in Asheville; Tony and Carol and
brood on vacation. When we connected by

phone, Chimney Rock seemed a perfect intermediary point.

We met at a local diner for breakfast then hiked to the viewing station atop Chimney Rock. For those who don't want to hike, you could park nearby and take an elevator up that chunk of rock to the top. You just had to be able to ascend the final steps to the viewing platform.

On this day a heavy-set fellow in a wheelchair came out of the elevator. Using arm brace crutches, he rose up near the bottom of the stairs. My brother Tony — as is his way — immediately ran to help. Tony's wife, Carol, took two-year-old Marissa while I watched over their three-year-old daughter Laurel.

Tony slung one of the guy's arms over his shoulders and proceeded upward, one hard-fought stair at a time. This young guy with dark hair — in his early twenties? — had great trouble moving his legs. Immediately, another man emerged from the crowd, lifting the young guy from the other side.

Together the three of them moved up step by step, the heavy-set young man exclaiming, "Help me, Jesus!" and "Thank you, Lord!" as they heaved upward.

I bent in toward Laurel's ear, whispering: "Look, Laurel, your Dad's a hero. All three of them are heroes. Remember this."

(I'm sure she doesn't; she was three.)

Impossibly interesting places abound everywhere! Impossibly interesting experiences can happen, if you're open to them. Today it takes the merest internet scan and you'll find them. Closer than you think, no matter where you are.

My favorite place is whichever sidewalk is beneath my feet because I am just constantly fascinated by walking and looking and learning.

~ Danny Meyer

Walking makes you a better lover

Yeahhhhhhh, made you look. Even if you were skimming through the segment headlines racing to the end….

Now that you're this far through *It Is Solved By Walking* I trust you've been stepping out, stepping up your walks, taking longer walks or more frequent walks. Because walking is sexy. Maybe even better than sex.

You're right — that's a bridge too far! Plus it would preclude my sequel *It Is Solved By Sex*.

It may not be better than sex, but that statement is in the neighborhood of truth, maybe even next door to it — walking makes you a better lover. Anything that improves your cardiovascular vitality enhances your ability to make love. Anything that makes your body fitter makes for a more sensual experience.

Also, if you think of walking metaphorically, lessons abound for romantic interludes. What do the best bring to their walks?

An open mind.

Curiosity.

Slowing things down to enjoy the languorous unfolding of sensation.

Stamina.

Rhythm.

Playfulness.

Who doesn't want those qualities in a lover?

If you do only one thing for your health, walk

Walking is man's best medicine.

~ Hippocrates

Anatomically today's humans are indistinguishable from humans several thousand years ago. Hippocrates is the Greek founder of modern medicine — all the accumulated data points of the past 2,500 years confirm what Hippocrates proposed, that there's no finer medicine than movement. Walking is the simplest form of exercise to undertake. We were designed for it.

In these pages we've noted the physical benefits of going for a walk.

There's a reason why walking speed is the top indicator — above all other indicators — for how long you have left to live.

There's a reason Dr. Dean Ornish makes an hour-long daily walk a pillar of his Reversing Heart Disease Without Drugs program.

It works!

Wonders.

"Eating a vegetarian diet, walking (exercising) everyday, and meditating is considered radical. Allowing someone to slice your chest open and graft your leg veins in your heart is considered normal and conservative."

~ Dr. Dean Ornish

You are here to live in radical good health, to spread radically good vibes, to live your vibrant best.

If you do only one thing to improve your vitality, go for a walk.

If you do only one thing to spur creative ideas, walk

If you are a thinker — a creator of any stripe — to forgo walking as a regular practice is to work against yourself. That cloaks off brain lightning — at least one broad avenue to it.

It's intriguing how the process works inversely to expectation. We think our best insights and most daring ideas will crackle forth while our brain is frothy with the electrical storm of intense work. But it's so often the opposite. It takes a becalmed mind *away from the work* to spark solutions. Genius even.

I am not a chef, but I've been forced to watch many a chefscapade on reality TV with my wife — I'm going to offer a cooking analogy, one I hope doesn't send foodies screaming to their kitchen knives:

Your work, your life, your projects, your entanglements, your art, your relationships — all the time and thought and energy you put into these vital aspects of your life are akin to prepping a meal — the sorting and cleaning, dicing and slicing, chopping and sprinkling and forming…. Those take effort. And time. And focus. And thought.

But is that what completes the meal? No! It's the slow burn in the oven or over the grill or in the pan. It's the heat, which requires so little of you, that brings it all together. You can walk away at that point. Whatever you've assembled is searing or steaming or frying or baking or bubbling or sizzling.

A walk is applied heat. You've worked hard at something. You've labored. You've deep dived. You've researched. You've exhausted yourself. Now it's time to apply some heat. It's time to walk away. Literally.

… Or nap or shower or make love or hop in the hammock or go for a drive or idle window-side on a train or soak in a tub or get a massage or listlessly listen to your Mom talk … I'm not going to pretend walks are the *only* way to let thoughts percolate …

It's time to let your thoughts simmer.

Know this: Walking sets the mind to simmer in a way few other activities do.

If you do only one thing to spur creative insight, to forward your progress, take a walk.

If you do only one thing to think more deeply about your life, walk

"Walking activates the primary motor cortex, which deals with initiation of action. It plays a role in how you get things done. It's why people pace when they're trying to think through a problem."

~ Mike Cohen, neurofeedback expert

Walking promotes brain-body coherence.

That walking jumpstarts the primary motor cortex suggests being in motion and problem solving have been yoked together since our evolutionary pre-history, since we ambled out in search of mammoths and mushrooms. Getting in motion to find solutions is an ancient practice. You can imagine how a predisposition to action would confer a survival advantage to early hominids. If a clan faced hunger, the simple act of moving would tip the odds in its favor for stumbling upon a food source. Once mobile, they would be scanning for game trails, searching the visible distance for fruit-bearing trees, puzzling out which direction might best lead to slugs and worms, nuts and berries.

Yes — feel free to take a moment to appreciate our modern grocery stores. Thankfully that experience still involves walking!

Though we're not burdened with acquiring food when we head out for a walk at this juncture in time, we are tasked with navigating the complexities of modern life. How efficient that our brain motor revs up, so we can grapple with that sneaky colleague at work. Or how we're going to find new clients. Better problems to have than sourcing larvae from fallen tree trunks.

More than creativity spur, more than mind and body optimizer, the ultimate joy in walking comes from connection. To people, to the natural world, to your hidden inner resources, to the Mystery itself. Committed walkers have felt this — that instance when all merges — your footsteps and breath and thoughts — and something else too — a pervading sense of unity. A moment when the walker is so fully immersed — so thoroughly absorbed — as to feel in tune with *all that is*. It's a fleeting and eternal feeling all at once. As though you are in a dance with all creation.

I and countless others have been gobsmacked by the profundity of existence while on a walk. It can come up slowly from a deep inner well or it can grab you so suddenly you gasp aloud.

If you do only one thing to summon insight into the workings of your life, take a walk.

It is solved by moving

Is walking the only solution? Of course not. Walking may not be for you on the regular. You may prefer sculling, biking, yoga, running, cross fit, weights, martial arts … In more demanding exercise expect solutions in the shower afterward.

I'm particularly keen on walking since I've added hiking poles to my walks. These poles of various weights make for a full-body exercise. In addition to the creative, bodily, mental and spiritual benefits, trekking poles add upper-body strengthening into the mix.

Walking — with poles in your hands — without sound in your ears — will flush body and spirit simultaneously.

Walking is transformation

"Above all, do not lose your desire to walk. Every day I walk myself into a state of well-being and walk away from every illness. I have walked myself into my best thoughts, and I know of no thought so burdensome that one cannot walk away from it.'"

~ **Soren Kierkegaard**, Danish philosopher

There is little that can't be transformed with a walk.

I went out for a walk and came back a better man

That first walk of my walking program on the heels of hospitalization — feeling oafish, sluggish, fattish — even then, the walk felt liberating. Feeling that death is stalking you in your own home has a way of focusing you. Thank God for that. It renewed a lifelong exploration by foot.

I was already walking our dog a few times a day. What I committed to was 45 minutes a day at a good clip by myself. With the dog it was stop and start every minute. He'd been cooped up for hours — it would have been cruel to march KaiDog fast and frenzied down the street. To let him explore the outer world at his own sniff-pee-amble-sniff pace — I owed him that. You and I speak. We read. We watch all manner of devices for our outer world information. Kai-Dog mainly has his sniffer. If he's not jamming his snout deep into the bush some other dog

235

peed on hours ago, he's not experiencing his world.

I went out for a walk and came back renewed.

I went out for a walk and came back with clarity.

I went out for a walk and returned bristling with ideas.

On a day of high anxiety, I went out for a walk and came back feeling grounded.

At a time when I was feeling scattershot, I went out for a walk and came back with a relaxed focus.

That first walk — fattish, sluggish, oafish — started a routine. Yes, over time my cardiovascular system improved. Yes, over time ideas sparked and I returned many a time brimming with possibility.

Most importantly, I went out for a walk — many a walk — and came back a better man. I came back to apologize to Ann for an insensitivity on my part. I came back vowing to improve in some capacity. I came back lighter — lighter-hearted — a better man to those around me, a better man to myself.

It's your turn now

First, let me speak to those of you who are in an awful place physically:

It may feel like trudgery at first — a slog — like you're moving through stretch wrap.

The best thing about walking is that you already do it. Even if you've let yourself go. You can start with a few extra steps.

My wife Ann went through cancer and an operation that left her depleted. She was exhausted and weak — she'd lost significant weight and much of her musculature. It was difficult to simply rise and stand.

Where did she start her resurgent comeback to the woman she is now? A few steps out our front door. I was her support mechanism. She shuffled down a couple steps to the sidewalk only a few feet away. We turned and ploddingly made it to the neighbor's property line. At the time we were living in a tight subdivision, every home crammed within a few feet of the others, so this was no leisurely country stroll. This was at most a 50-foot walk.

Then we turned around. She made it back, collapsed onto a couch … and vowed never to move again.

The next day she went a little further.

You can too.

Fast forward and just last year she caught the 10,000 steps a day craze. She had her FitBit on —

Even if you've not done a single physical activity for years, you can do this. Just start. Taking yourself out for a walk is the most wonderful thing — just open that front door and venture forth.

Now let me speak to all of you.

You're here reading this because you're creative beings in a challenging environment, seeking easy ways to be your optimal best. Now you know — walking solves *everything*!

If you are getting exercise already several times a week and want to increase your mobility, try adding a morning walk, an evening walk, a midday walk during your lunch break.

If you haven't already begun a walking program, start today.

What?! Are you still sitting here reading this bookito? Get up already — get out — go for a walk!

If you have only one practice, make it walking.

It is meditation, exercise, transformation and idea spur rolled into one activity.

If you do only one thing, walk.

(!)

It is the best of humanity,
I think, that goes out to walk.

~ Ralph Waldo Emerson

The End (with a link for more)

I'm honored you read this bookito. Thank you!

If you enjoyed the material here, please consider leaving a brief review. Reviews on Amazon and Goodreads (and elsewhere!) are the lifeblood for today's writers.

More than that, I hope you stay in touch. If you want more (free) creative spirit info and would like to be notified when new books come out, sign up for the Oh So Occasional Email Newsletter here:

http://www.notesforcreators.com/join-email/

Bonus material:

Just Keep Walking by Minx Boren

Just keep walking.
Walk for the health of it.
Walk for the exuberance of it.
Walk to feed your spirit
and to uplift your soul.

Walk away from what no longer
serves you…or others.
Walk toward what inspires you.
Walk toward what you can do…
toward what you find compelling
and meaningful and worthwhile.

Walk out from under any shadows
or shoulds that could weigh you down.

Walk out beyond limitations and the grief

that lingers after loss.

Walk way beyond your comfort zone

And take giant strides toward your best self.

Walk on and on and on

with hope in your heart

and love on your mind

and a lively and enlivening spring

in your every step.

Move more and more fully

into your life.

Enjoy the journey.

Thankfulness

Thank you, Dan Richards. Every writer needs an editor. To have a damn fine editor and a life-long friend wrapped into one, does it get any better than this?! You get what I'm trying to communicate, even when I mangle it.

Thank you, Laura Duffy, for the impactful cover design. Barack Obama! Deepak Chopra! So many others of note — and now my little bookito — I feel like I've finally found my designer-for-life. (You can find her at LauraDuffyDesign.com.)

Thank you to EbookLaunch.com for making the interior digital design sing.

Thank you, love of my life!

Thank you, joy boy! (Now bigger 'n' stronger than me.) (Finally.)

Thank you, Sebson! (It's heartening to see you pursuing a path of personal growth as you enter adulthood.)

Thank you, family, for making this existence a party whenever you're around. MomJo! Tony and Carol! Keefus! Char and Char! (The first is pronounced with a *sh*; the second is pronounced with a *ch* — Charlene and Charlie).

And you too, next generation: Laurel and Marissa and Nicole and Noelle. Lily and Kyle and Kendall. And George.

Thank you, Travis Thomas. I'm lifted by your example of living a modern-day Dao. Your mission to infuse the essence of improvisation into everyday philosophy inspires me. (Check out LiveYesAnd.com, if only to find out what the hell that means.) (And how engaging the mantra at the heart of improv comedy guides you nimbly through quagmires and successes alike.)

Thank you, Brain Reekers, my accountability partner. Our weekly confabs have propelled this bookito into reality. More than that, I value *your questions*. Even morer than that, I value our friendship.

Thank you, Breakfast Boys Club. Mike Cohen and Scott Doyle — sharing Sunday morning insights with you guys is the linchpin of my week. Between the cutting edge of science and health (Mike) and charmed life adventures (Scott), I think we have the gamut of experience covered. As this goes to publication in the time of coronavirus, I'm missing the endcap to my week with both of you!

Thank you, Guy Hoffman, you and I have the tastiest of creative spirit conversations always. It's a thrill to delight in the delight of this existence with you.

Thank you, Carolyn — you live openly and brazenly what many of us aspire to live privately. Your spirit-connected way is refreshing.

Thank you, Minx-a-lot — that's Minx Boren, who in her mid-70s accomplishes more than most millennials. That's not a dig on millennials — I'm just sayin' she's got more projects in the air than people half her age. What a whirlwind of exploration she is. Check her out at CoachMinx.com. Check out that photo — that's her! That's who she is. An energetic perceptive bundle of good friendship and keen insight.

Thank you, KMom — for adopting me into your family of the heart. You're an example of creative spirit going strong — in your mid-80s! (If you're into animal sculpture, check out Kate VanNoorden's work.)

Thank you, Studio E team past and present — to work side by side with people you admire makes for funtastic days. Kris, thanks for lending your wizard ops art ninja skills to the gallery. Your steadfast equanimity in times good and bad keeps us all zen. Julian, here's to Soul Kontrol! You live it, you badass of free flowingness. Roseann, I miss the pre-covid days when we worked each week side by side in that cramped office space — thanks for being the unseen seam making for a (mostly) seamless operation. And to you especially, Dan Cella — for your unflagging commitment to bettering the art gallery, for your multi-capable ways, and most most most for the wit and laughter.

Damn, you make me laugh. LOLAL. Really truly out loud a lot.

Thank you, Rick Eggert, glass blower of exceptional talent and latest newest breakfast buddy. Love the mix of art and spirit we fling over eggs and potatoes.

Thank you, Pablo Diablo — You walked into our gallery as a client and have ended up as a good good friend.

Thank you, Tamaniac — You are the artist I've spoken with most over the years. It's like being given a powerful telescope into the creative process. Your relentless quest for better never subsides.

Thank you, T-chele — I've valued your keen business acumen and your spiritual insights equally. How lucky for me and Ann to get both in one package.

Thank you to my forever friends:

Gil, for the eternal conversation — mostly on walks! Many don't have a daily friend, we do, we're lucky. Talky talk is underrated for solving all of a dude's issues for the moment.

Ras, for your sanctuary when I'm on the road. Living in the heart of the South as you do, however reluctantly, has made your place my home away from home. I've relished our episodic communions, where we get deep, raw, expansive and silly in turns.

Lo, for check-ins when you're en route: Montana to Florida; Florida to Montana. Oh, and when I'm traveling too. I'm not sure we know how to converse without road noise in our ears.

Thank you, G-Force. David and Sue, you have inspired us from the beginning. No one demonstrates it like you. You guys are the blueprint. Your creativity, grit and make-me-blow-ice-tea-through-my-nose hilarity (mostly you, Sue, mostly you) have helped make this creative journey such a rich one. Thanks for being our compadres in the art life.

This appreciation fest is going to be longer than the bookito itself if I keep this up. Thank you to all the rest who've made this path so immensely intensely enjoyable. Every connection, every conversation, every shared moment — hallelujah for them all! And you …

OmJah, thank You for this eternal Yumi adventure.

Additional resources

Books are long lived — like you on walking! Articles and scientific studies have shorter lifespans. Even so, in addition to books, I've included articles and studies here that will deepen your understanding.

Since many links deactivate over time as new information comes to the fore, even in the ebook version I'm not including links. I am, though, including enough keywords with each resource that a quick internet search should easily get you there.

For those of you with itchy fingers and a mad desire to learn more pronto, searching the phrase 'benefits of walking' will start you in the right direction for all you might want to know.

Listed here are resources pertaining to the art and science of walking:

Wanderlust: A History of Walking

Rebecca Solnit

The curious person's compendium on everything walking. Philosophy, anthropology, memoir. Detailed dives into gardens, labyrinths, the wild, the urban, and the mundane — if there's anything she missed pertinent to the history of walking, it's not for lack of curiosity and dogged determination to include it all. This is a colossal effort, well worth the time for anyone interested in exhaustive research about all things ambulatory.

Wild: From Lost to Found on the Pacific Coast Trail

Cheryl Strayed

She set foot on the trail addicted and broken; she left it engaged with life again. If there's only one memoir you read this year, make it this one. Few mine their experience as deeply and hauntingly and engagingly as Strayed does.

Tales of a Female Nomad: Living at Large in the World

Rita Golden Gelman

Walking

Henry David Thoreau, an essay

Reveries of a Solitary Walker

Jean-Jacques Rousseau, 10 essays on the experience of walking, not all of them completed before his death. To be clear, he didn't finish any of them after his death.

How To Walk

Thich Nhat Hanh: A series of brief meditations on mindful walking.

Daily Rituals: How Artists Work

Mason Currey

While not about walking per se, if you're a creative you will relish diving into the workaday routines of some of history's greatest minds. Walking looms large for many of these creators. As noted at the beginning of *It Is Solved By Walking*, it was Mason Currey's book that first startled me into recognizing how pervasive walking is for world-class creators.

Hemingway, Thoreau, Jefferson and the Virtues of a Good Long Walk

Arianna Huffington

An article in The Huffington Post on walking for health, for mental acuity and for creative problem solving.

Dr. Dean Ornish's Program for Reversing Heart Disease: The Only System Scientifically Proven to Reverse Heart Disease Without Drugs or Surgery

It's a mouthful, this title and subtitle, but a tasty plant-based one. One pillar of this program is the beneficial effects of walking a minimum of half an hour a day, ideally an hour a day.

The Deadliest Sin

Jonathan Shaw, Harvard Magazine article

From survival of the fittest to staying fit just to survive: scientists probe the benefits of exercise — and the dangers of sloth.

Weight loss success stories from walking

WalkAtHome.com

The emphasis is on walking inside your home, so you're never thwarted by heat, cold, rain, sleet, snow, or the fear of running into a verbose neighbor.

How 3 Women Walked Off 140 Pounds

Prevention Magazine article

Search: Prevention Magazine walk-your-butt-off

Walking speed predicts life expectancy of older adults

Scientific American Magazine article

Study: Gait speed and survival among older adults

Journal of the American Medical Association

JAMANetwork.com

Study result: "More steps taken per day are associated with lower mortality rates until approximately 7500 steps."

JAMANetwork.com article:

Association of Step Volume and Intensity With All-Cause Mortality in Older Women

Study: 10,000 steps not a magic number for fitness

Harvard.edu article of the same name.

Exercise: Improve your health, mood, and cognitive function

and

Sitting disease is the new health hazard

Articles of the same name on PepperPerspective.com

Erik Peper, Professor of Holistic Health

Study: Amount of time spent in sedentary behaviors and cause-specific mortality in US adults

By these researchers:

Charles E Matthews, Stephanie M George, Steven C Moore, Heather R Bowles, Aaron Blair, Yikyung Park, Richard P Troiano, Albert Hollenbeck, and Arthur Schatzkin

Review: The Effects of Acute Exercise on Mood, Cognition, Neurophysiology, and Neurochemical Pathways

Authors:

Julia C. Basso and Wendy A. Suzuki

Center for Neural Science, New York University, New York, NY, USA

Weight-Loss Transformations: How I Walked Myself Slim

By Karen Asp, Woman's Day Magazine

"Greater amounts of walking are associated with greater gray matter volume, which is in turn associated with a reduced risk of cognitive impairment."

Conclusion from 9-year study in Neurology.org:

Physical activity predicts gray matter volume in late adulthood

The positive effect on creative thinking (almost an outtake)

American Psychological Association article (APA.org)

Give Your Ideas Some Legs: The Positive Effect of Walking on Creative Thinking

Text in quotations below are from this article (the rest of the text is mine):

From a 2014 Stanford study co-authored by Marily Oppezzo, a Stanford doctoral graduate in educational psychology, and Daniel Schwartz, a professor at Stanford Graduate School of Education:

"People have noted that walking seems to have a special relation to creativity. The philosopher Friedrich Nietzsche (1889) wrote, "All truly great thoughts are conceived by walking" (Aphorism 34). The current research puts such observations on solid footing. Four studies demonstrate that walking increases creative ideation. The effect is not simply due to the increased perceptual stimulation of moving through an environment, but rather it is due to walking. Whether one is outdoors or on a treadmill, walking improves the generation of novel yet appropriate ideas, and the effect even extends to when people sit down to do their creative work shortly after."

The authors are careful to make a distinction between divergent thinking (coming up with novel ideas) and convergent thinking (focused problem solving). You wouldn't head out for a walk to solve a mathematical equation, though you might consider taking a walk to get a fresh flow of ideas about a mathematics principle.

To be more specific: Real creativity is not involved in convergent thinking. Convergent thinking is coming up with standard answers to what is already known — like you might find on a multiple-choice test. When you take a driver's license exam they're not looking for creative interpretation of road rules. They want to ascertain how well you know The Rules, not how clever you might be in making your own.

As creative beings, we're after divergent thinking. The holy grail of thought. Thought that moves us forward into new territory. Mickey Mouse, calculus, your digital everything device, every pop song you can't get out of your head, *Eat Pray Love*, plumbing, hot dogs, howitzers, how to get that love interest to glance your way, kites….

All these, when first dreamed up, broke new ground. Something new was created that did not exist before. Divergent thinking is creative thinking. Thinking that diverges from rote mental pathways.

Oppezzo and Schwartz note:

"Walking had a large effect on creativity. Most of the participants benefited from walking compared with sitting, and the average increase in creative output was around 60%. When walking, people also generated more uses, good and bad."

Whether participants walked outdoors or indoors on a treadmill, it didn't matter. Either way, idea flow was enhanced. (However, other studies show memory is better improved by nature walks than urban.)

"Walking is an easy-to-implement strategy to increase appropriate novel idea generation. When there is a premium on generating new ideas in the workday, it should be beneficial to incorporate walks."

Ah, yes, go for a walk! Get the crackle of electricity strumming across your neural net.

"In addition to providing performance benefits, it would address concerns regarding the physiological effects of inactivity."

That too. Especially.

PS: You're going to appreciate this — about the origin of the Stanford walking and creativity studies. Says Marily Oppezzo:

"My doctoral advisor [Daniel Schwartz] had the habit of going for walks with his students to brainstorm. One day we got kind of meta."

Yes, *they were on a walk!* Walks frequently taken by Schwartz specifically to facilitate the flow of ideas.

Take a Walk: The Work & Life Benefits of Walking

Ryan Holiday (RyanHoliday.net)

I came across this article after I'd finished writing *It Is Solved By Walking*. Even though it didn't influence this particular project, this is a superb post by a compelling thinker. I must include it!

(If you've not yet discovered Ryan Holiday, pick up a book of his, any book, you'll be hooked.)

Made in United States
North Haven, CT
04 September 2024